Pirates
Coloring Book

Adult Colouring Books

Aryla Publishing 2017

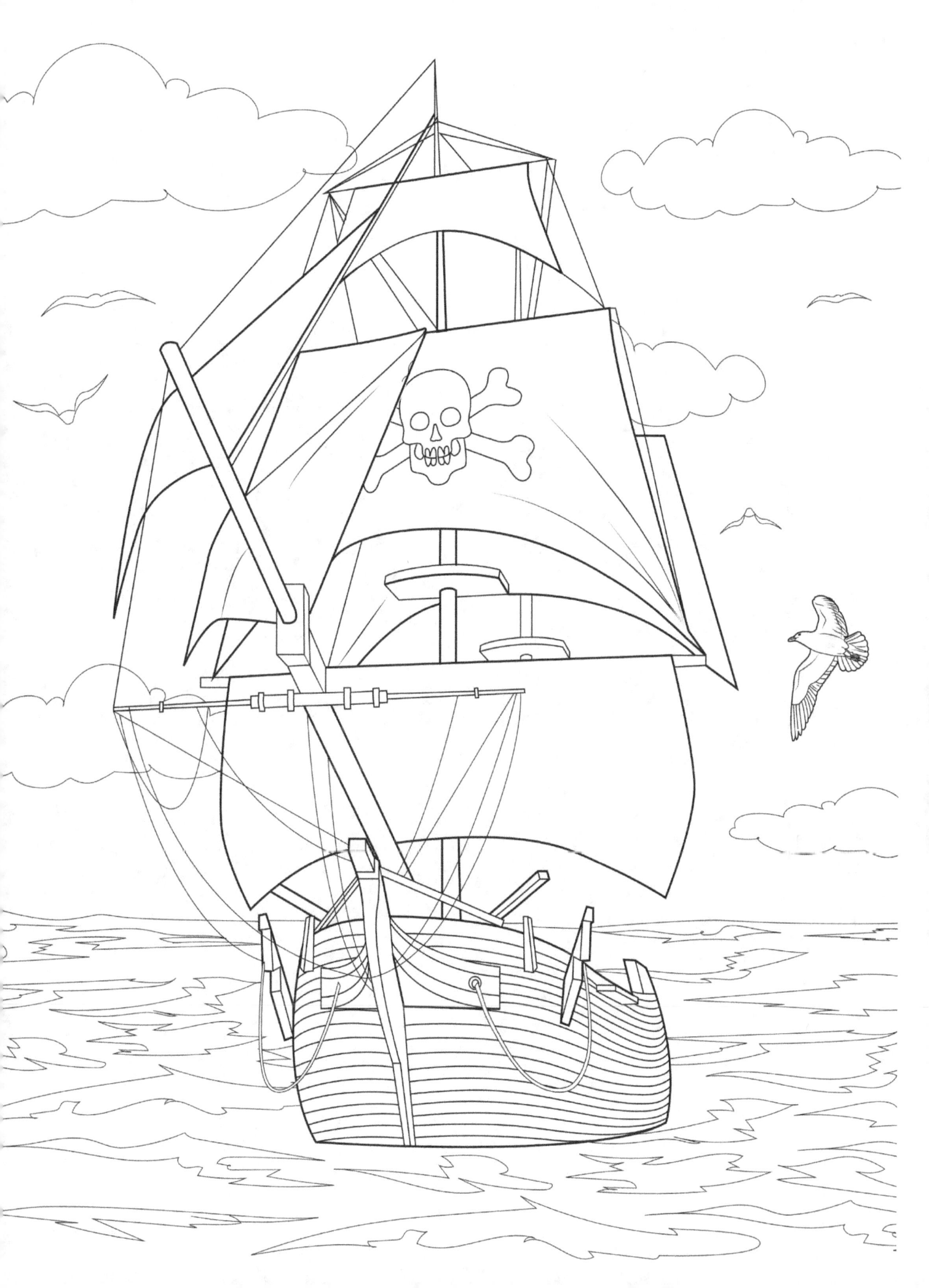

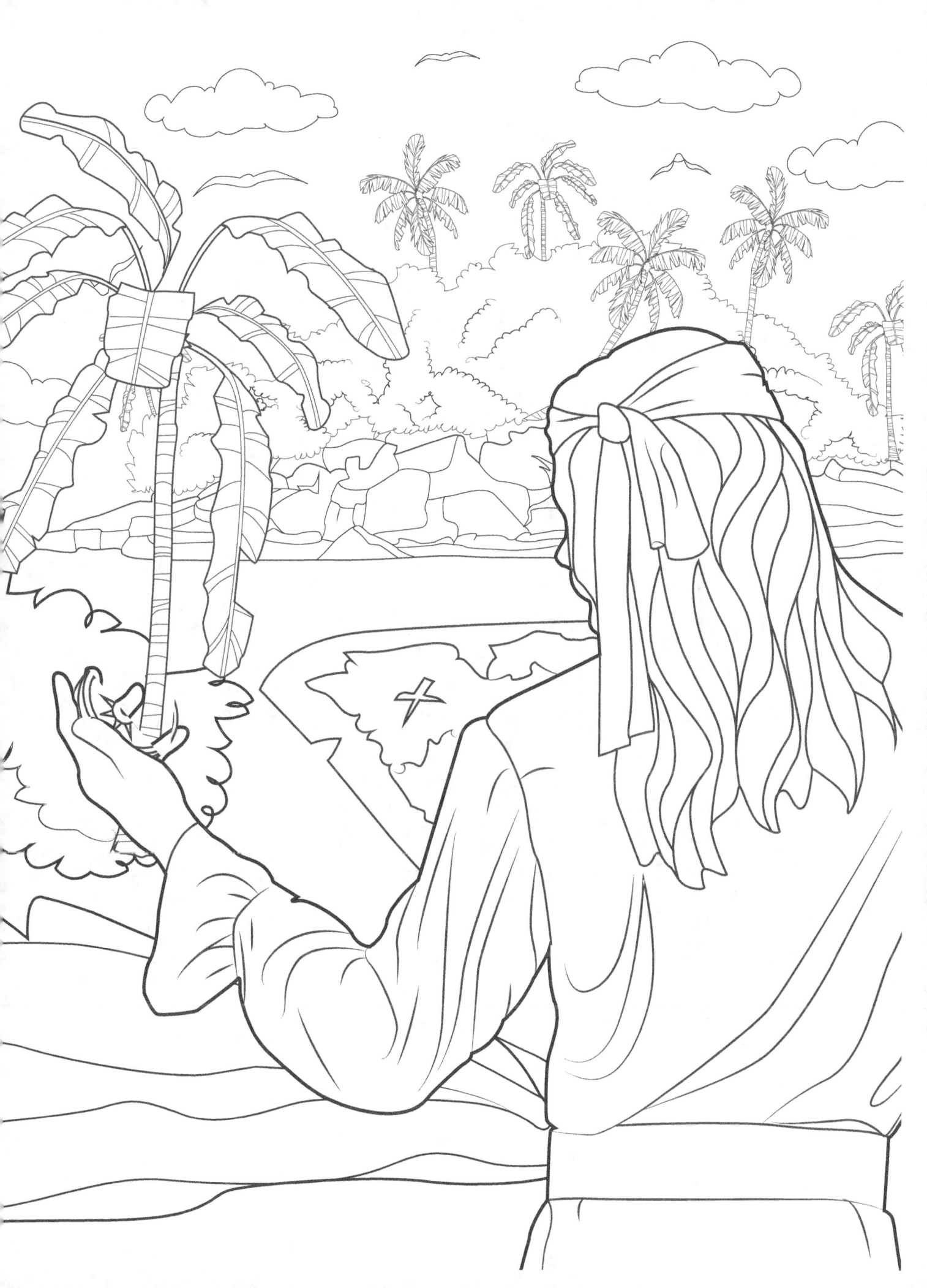

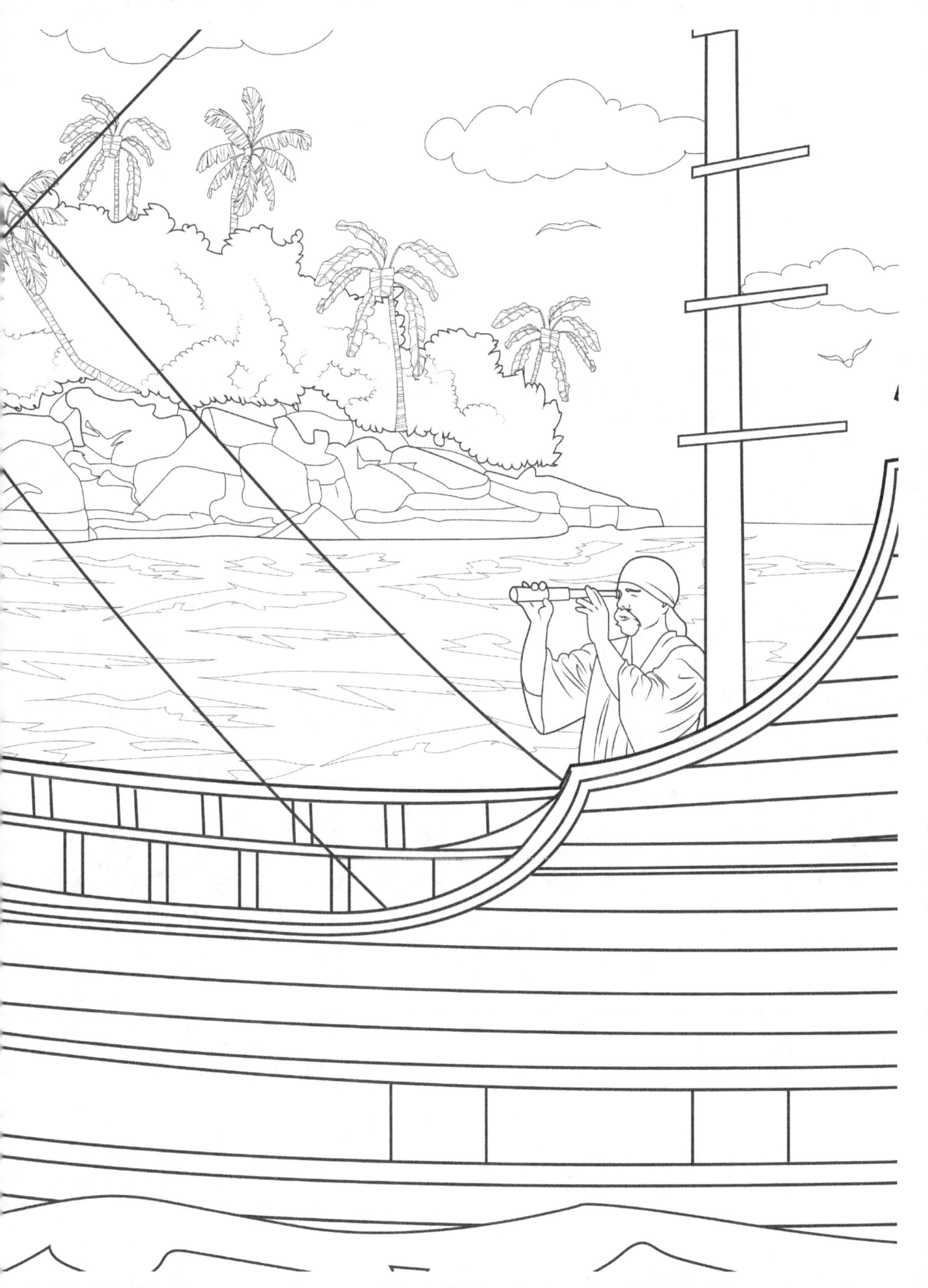

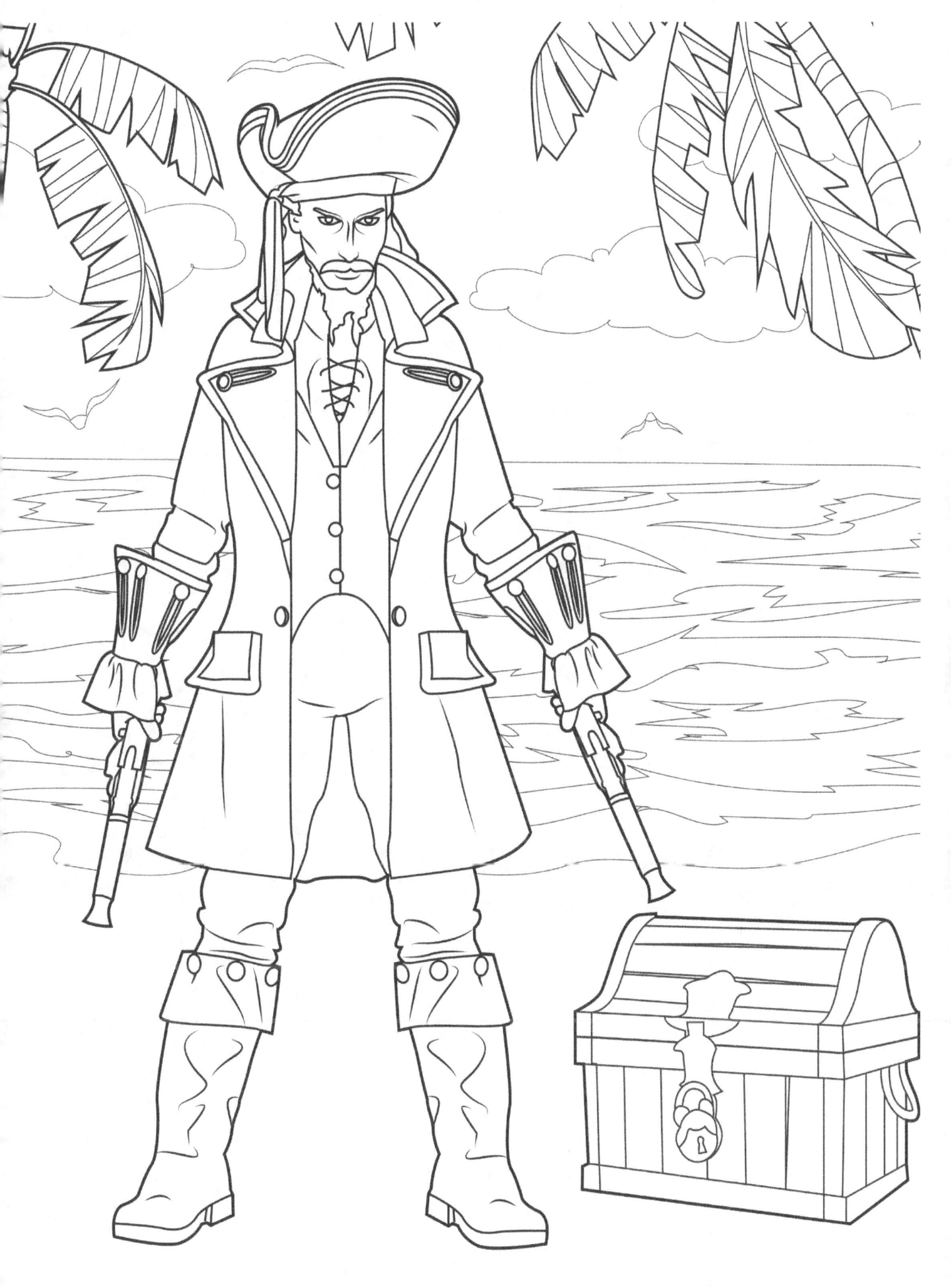

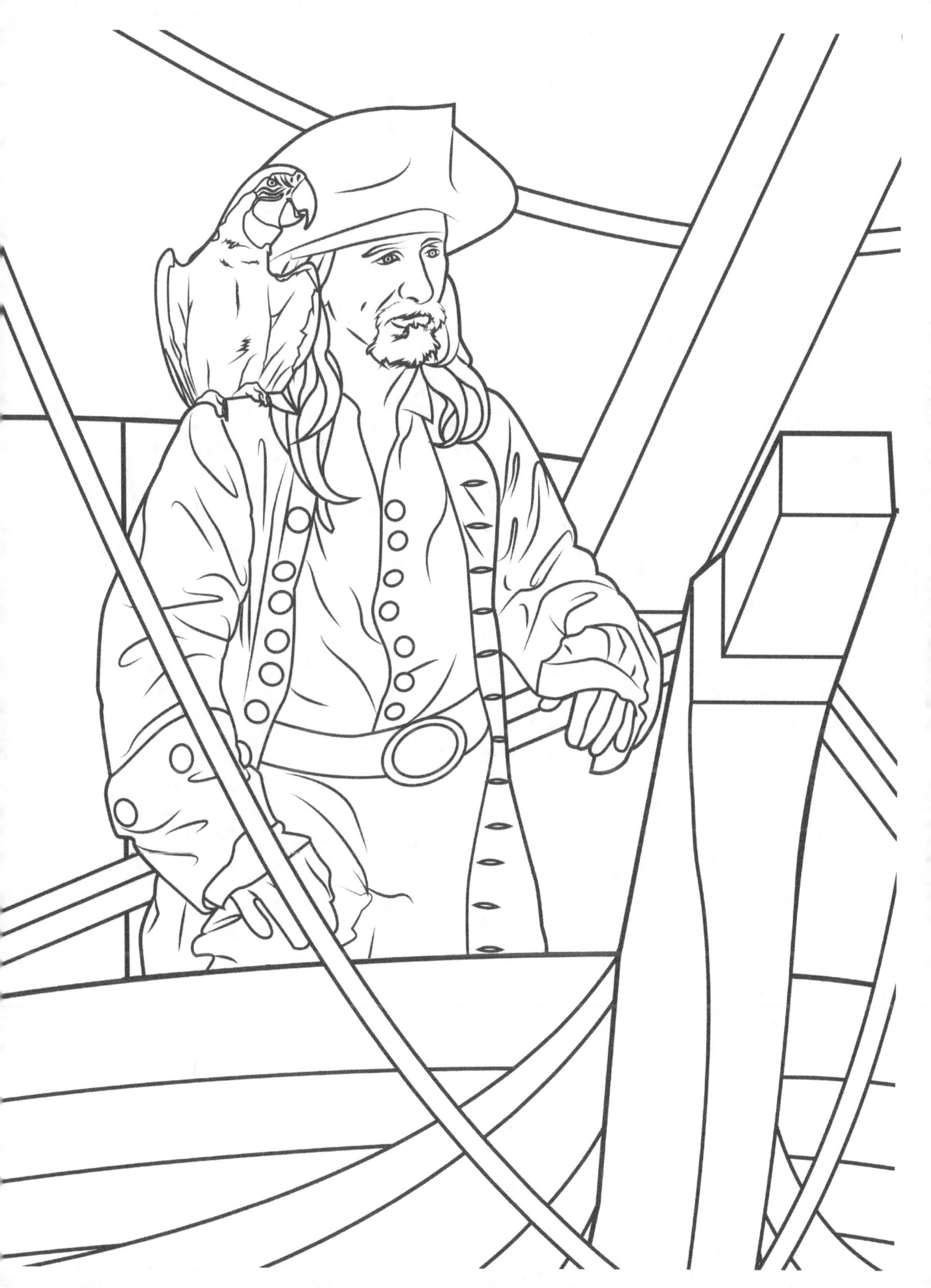

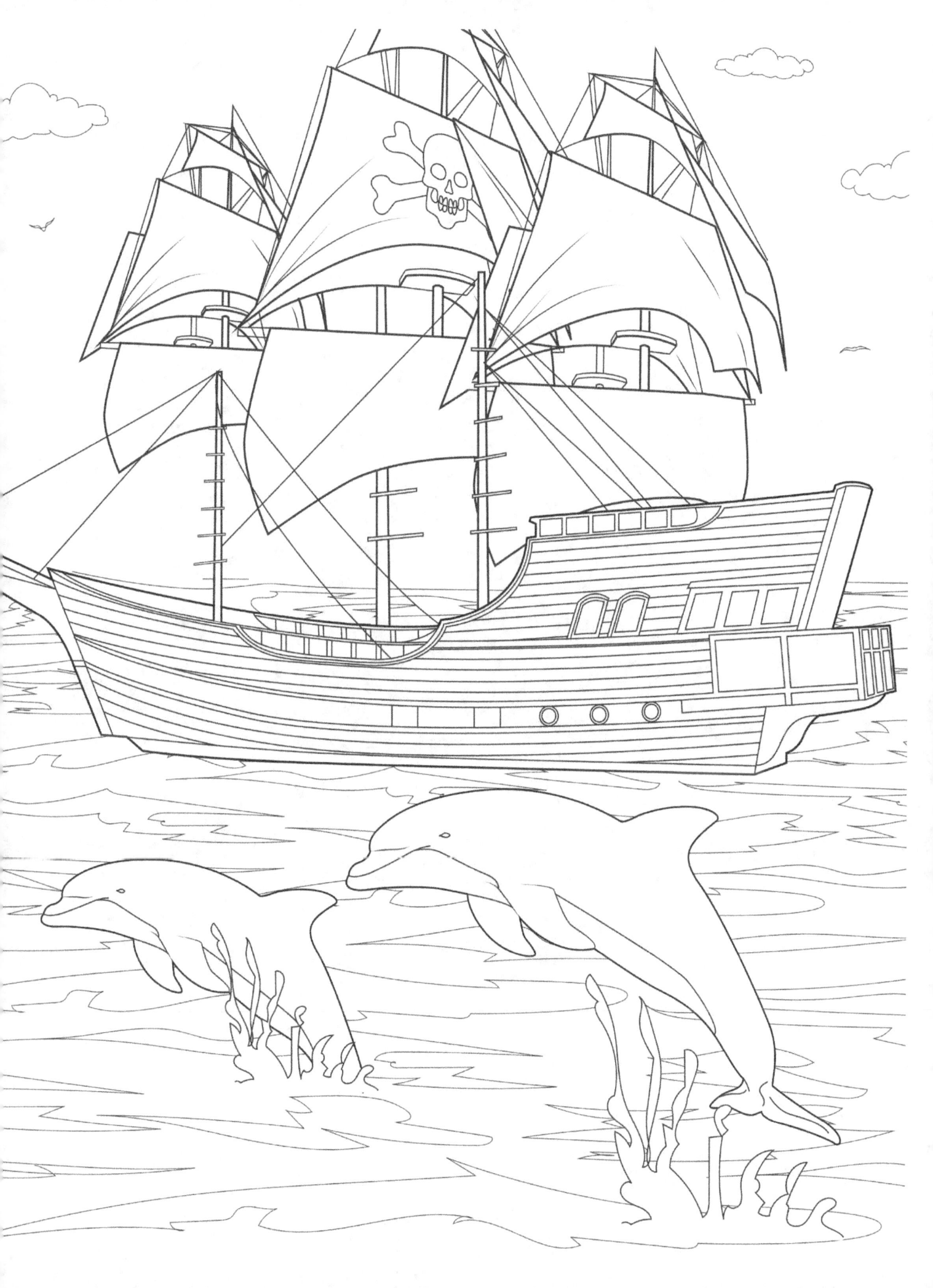

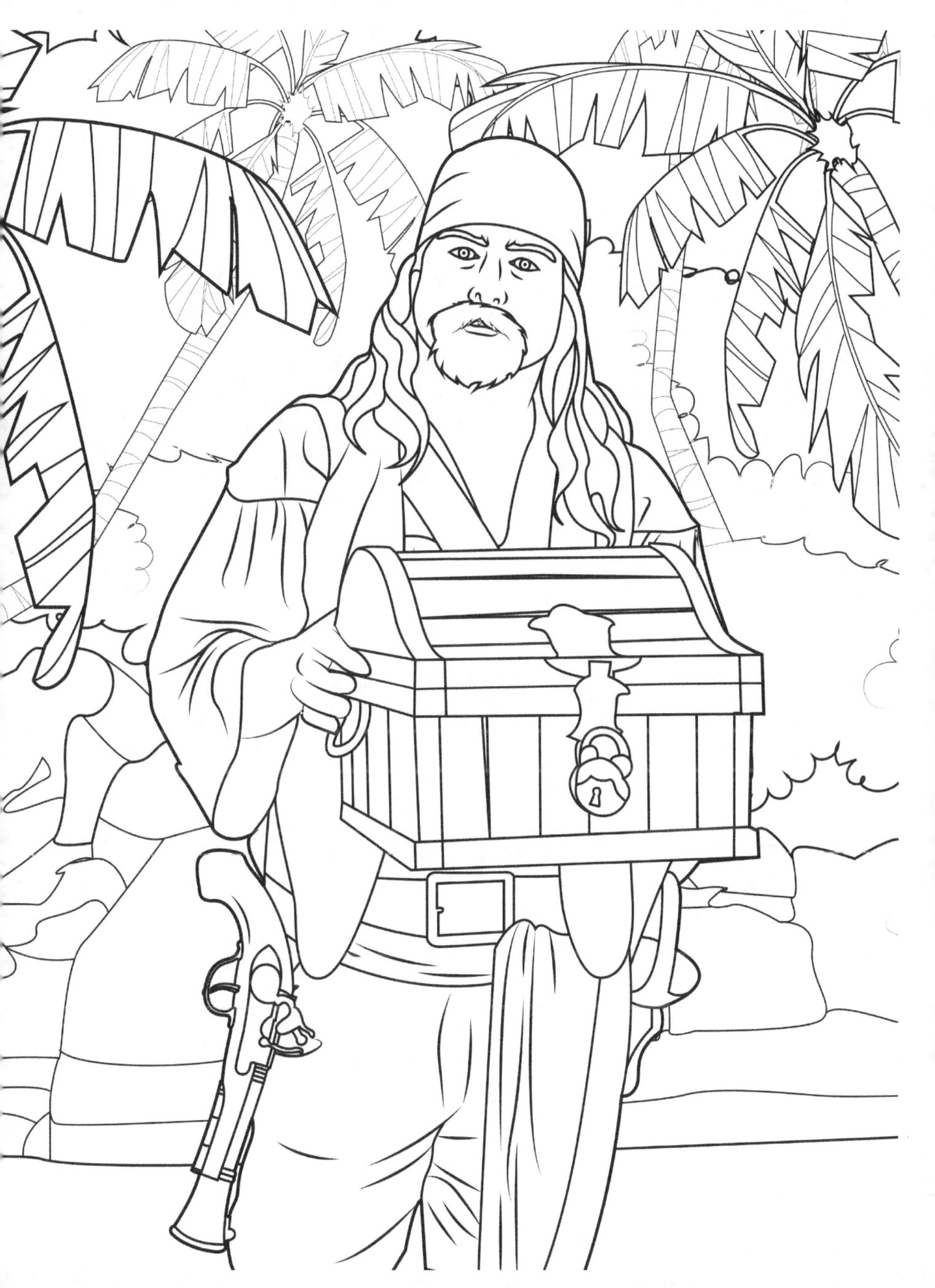

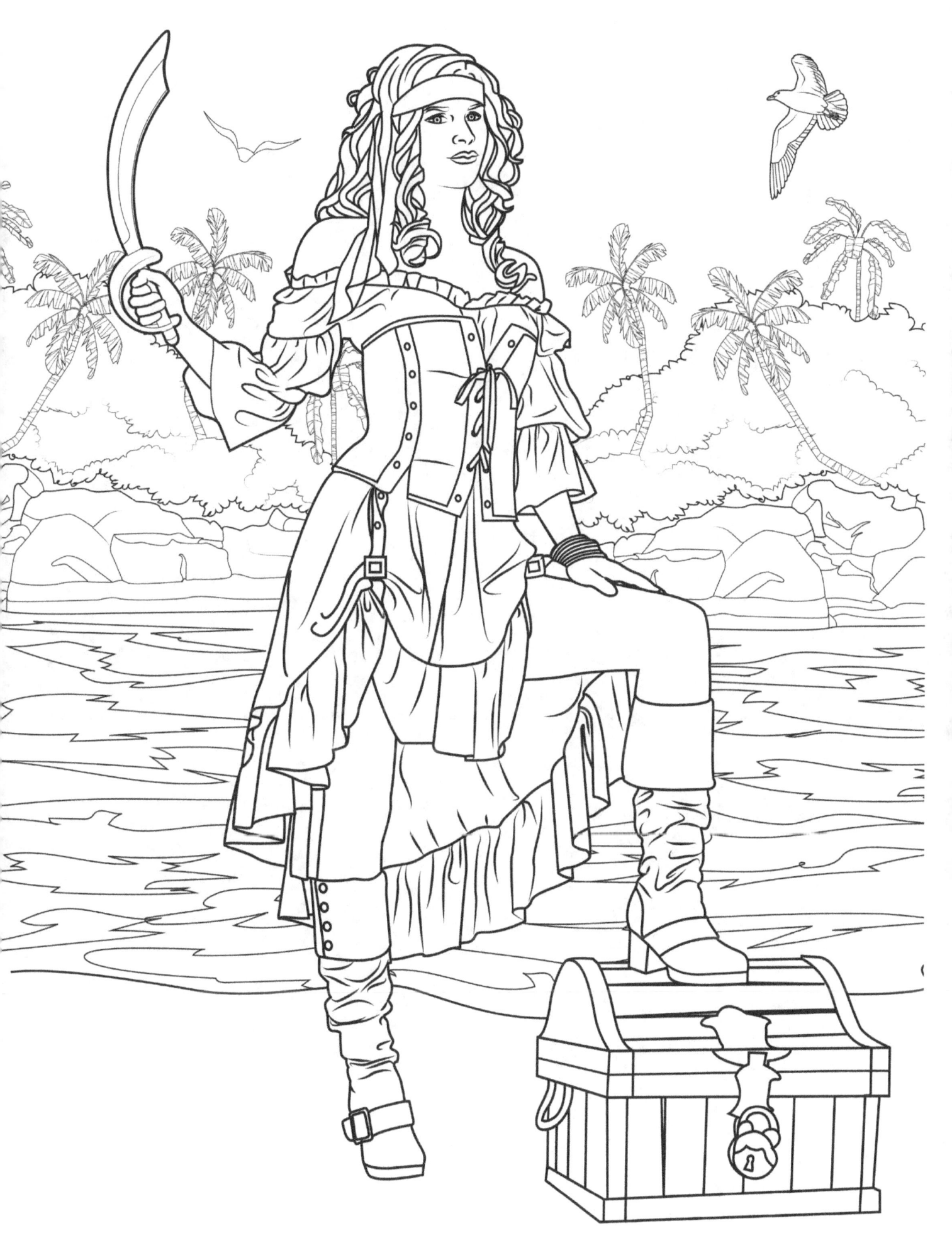

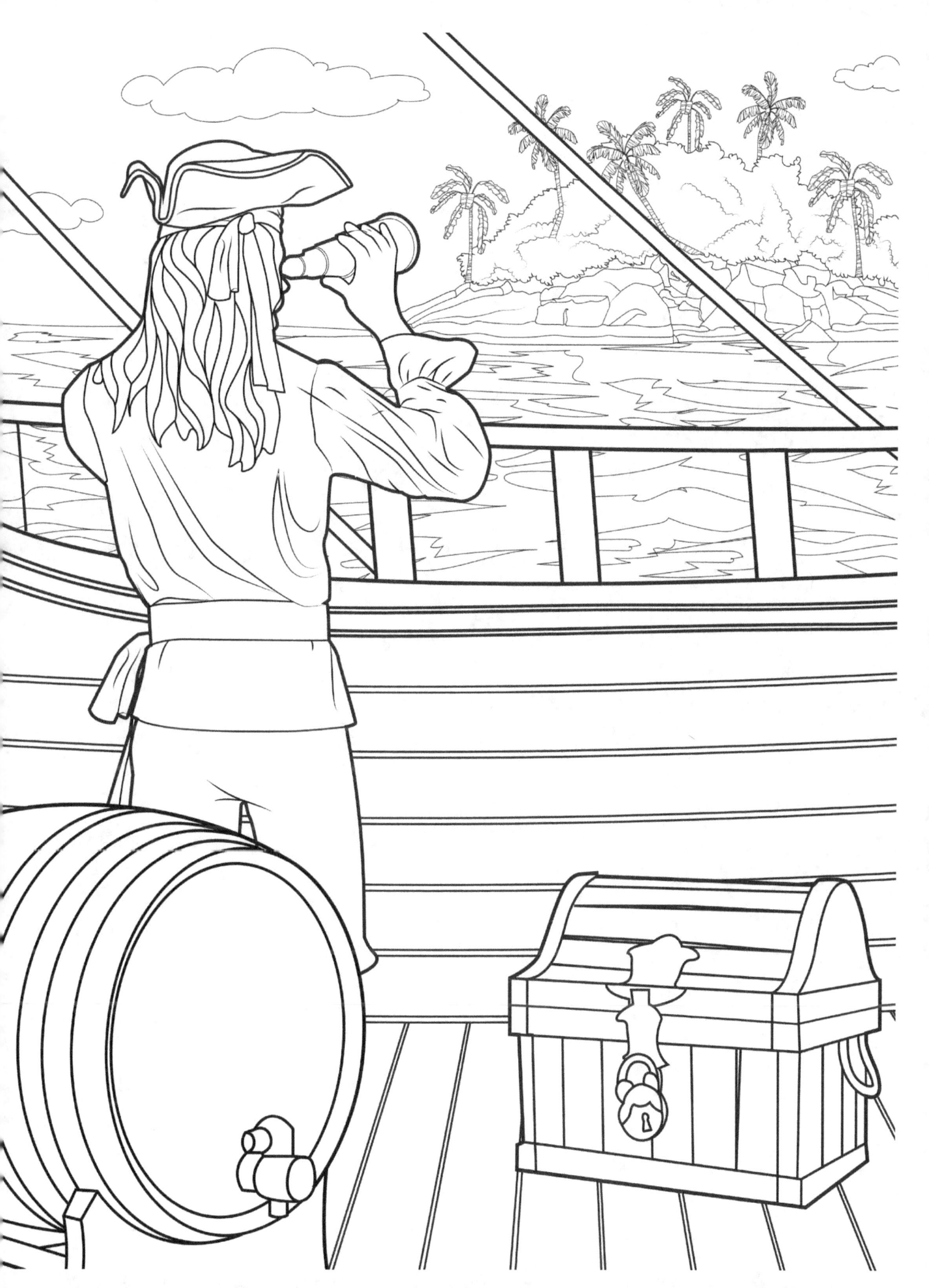

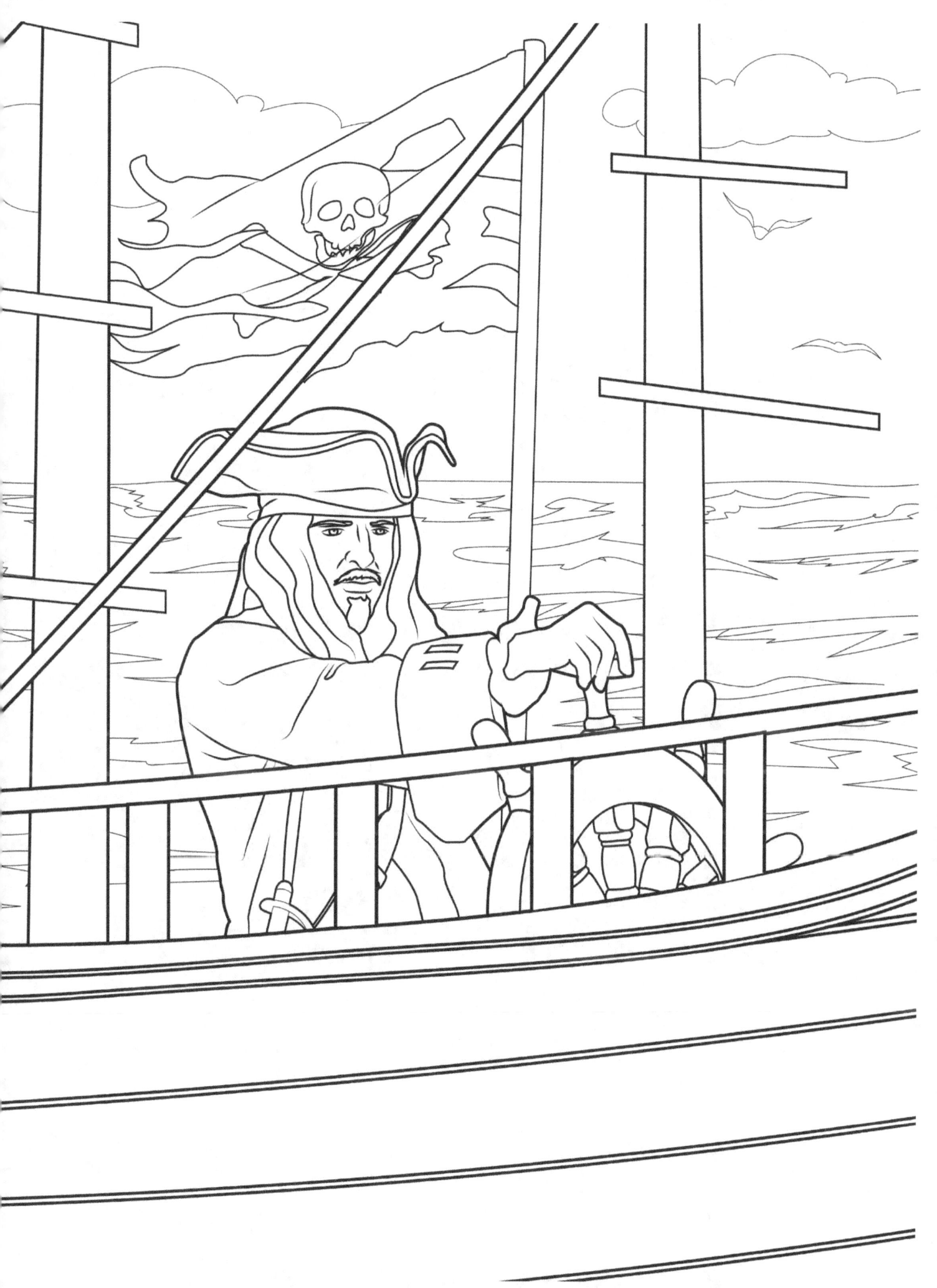

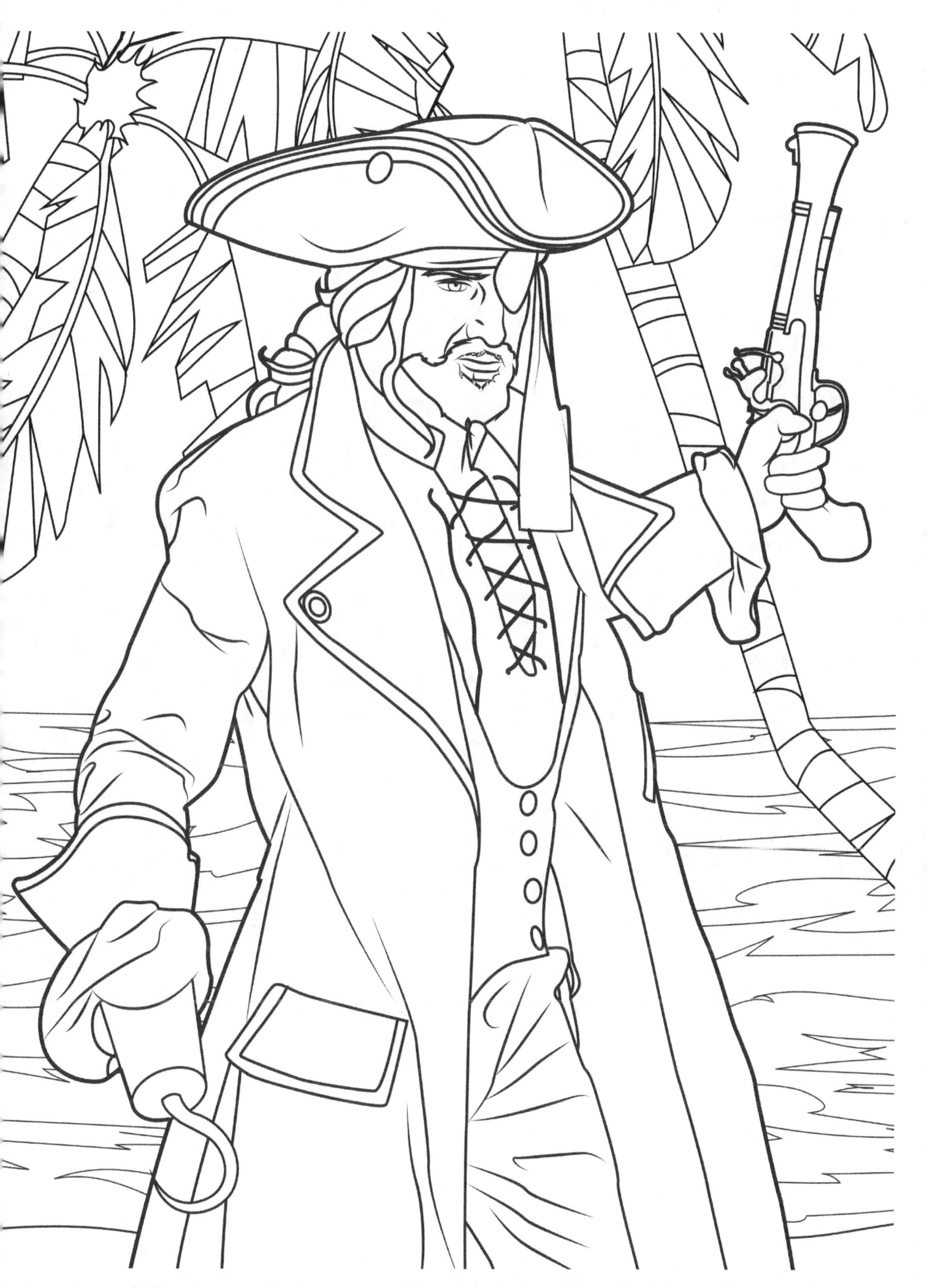

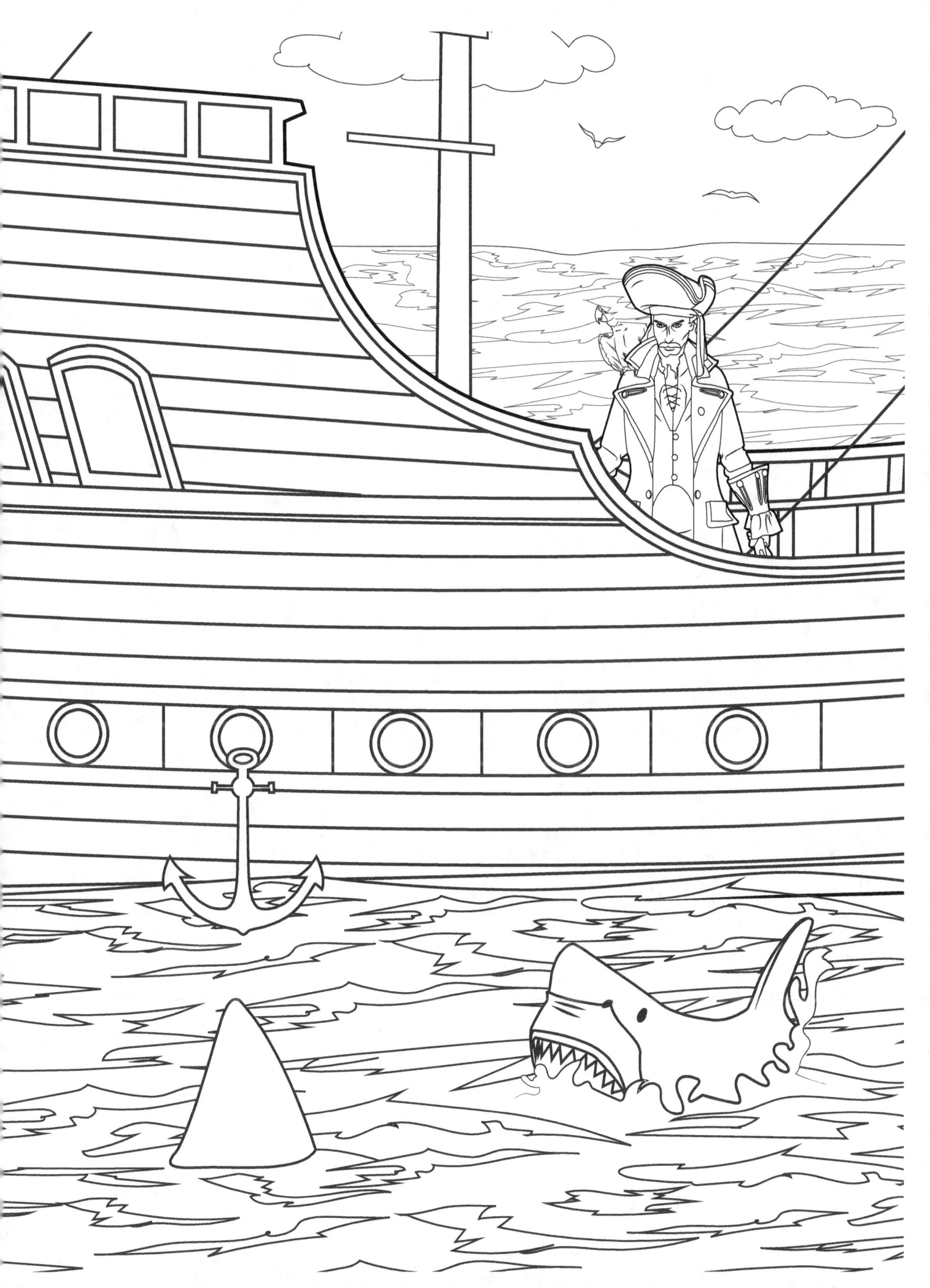

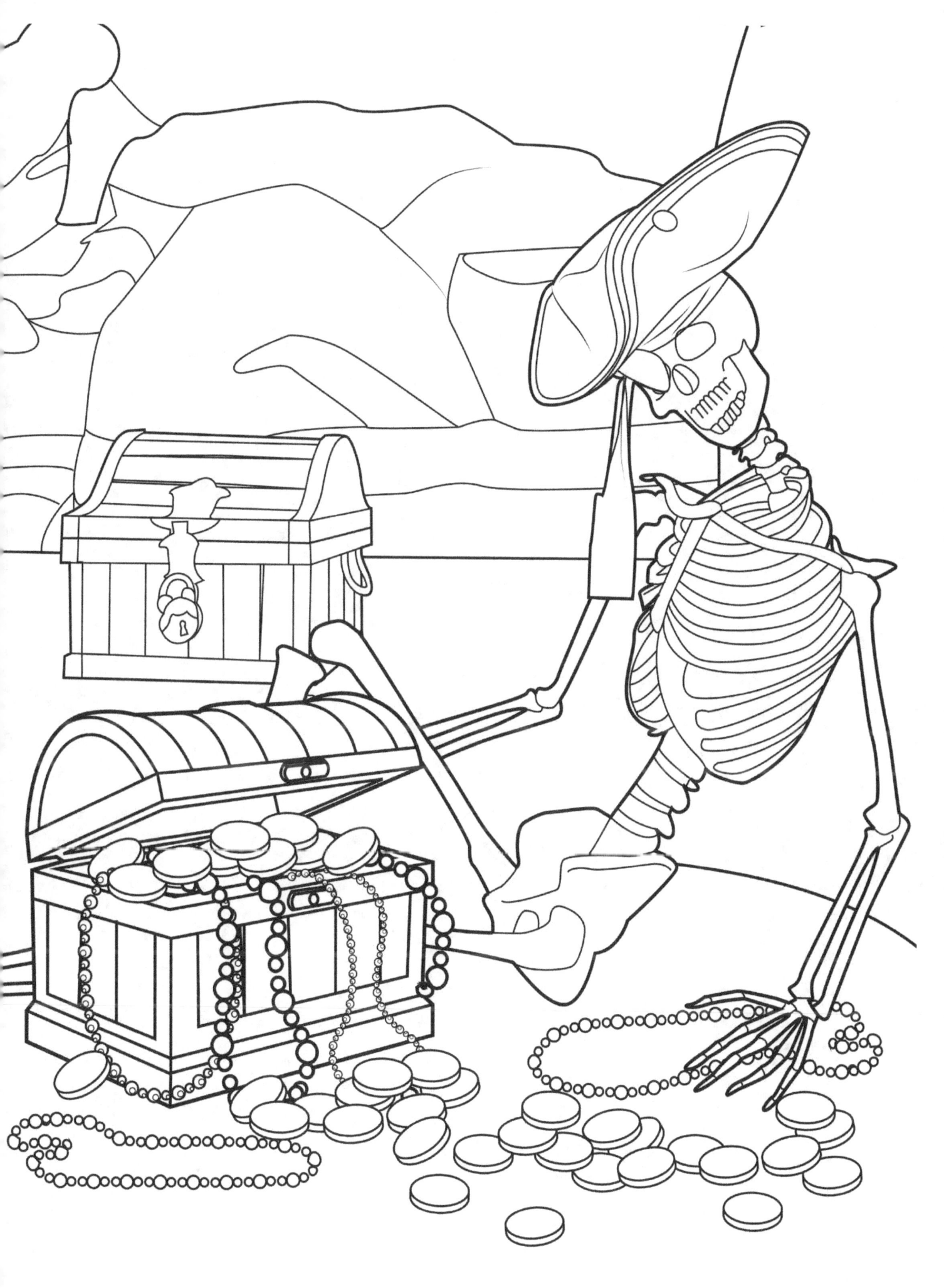

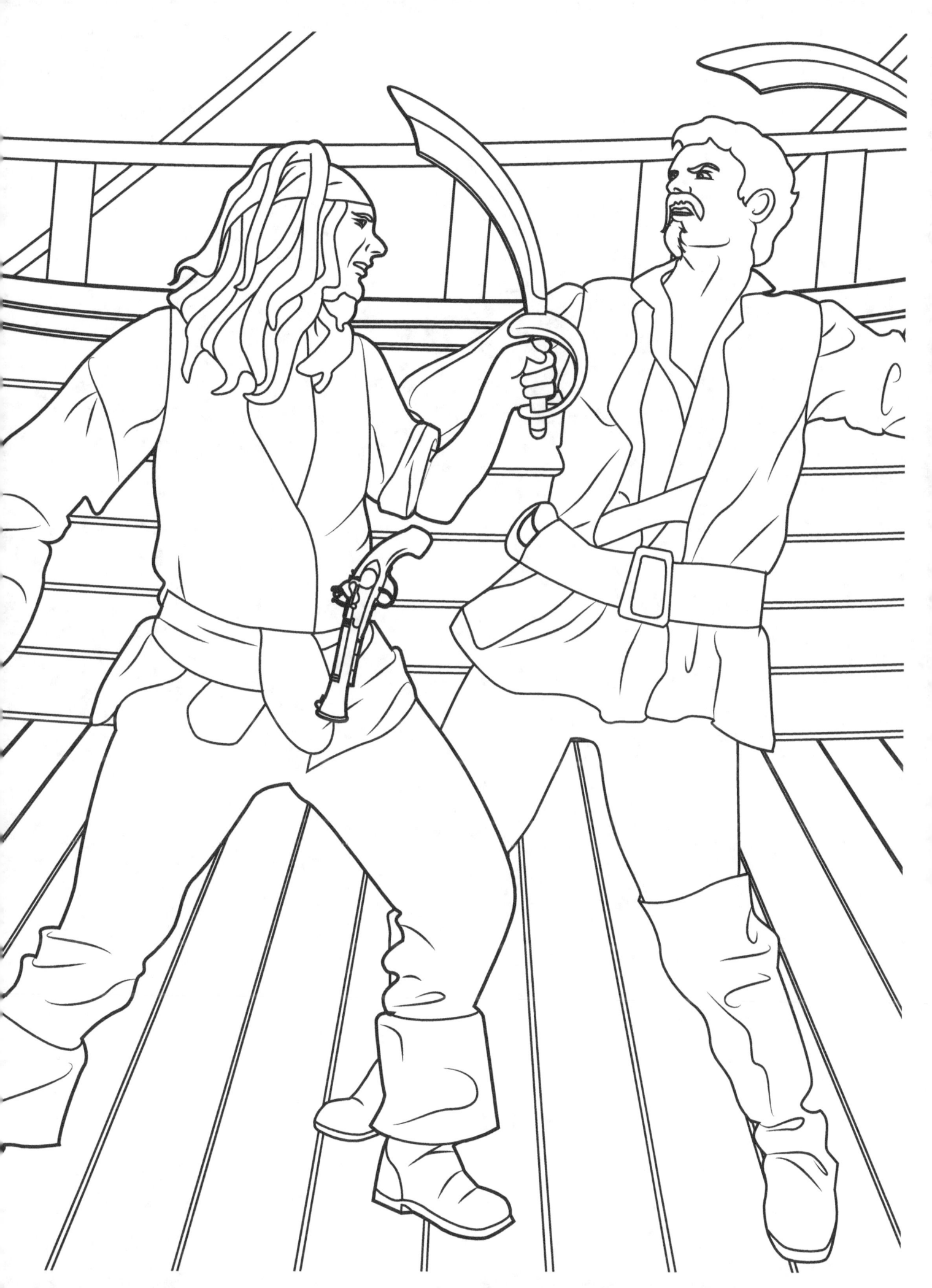

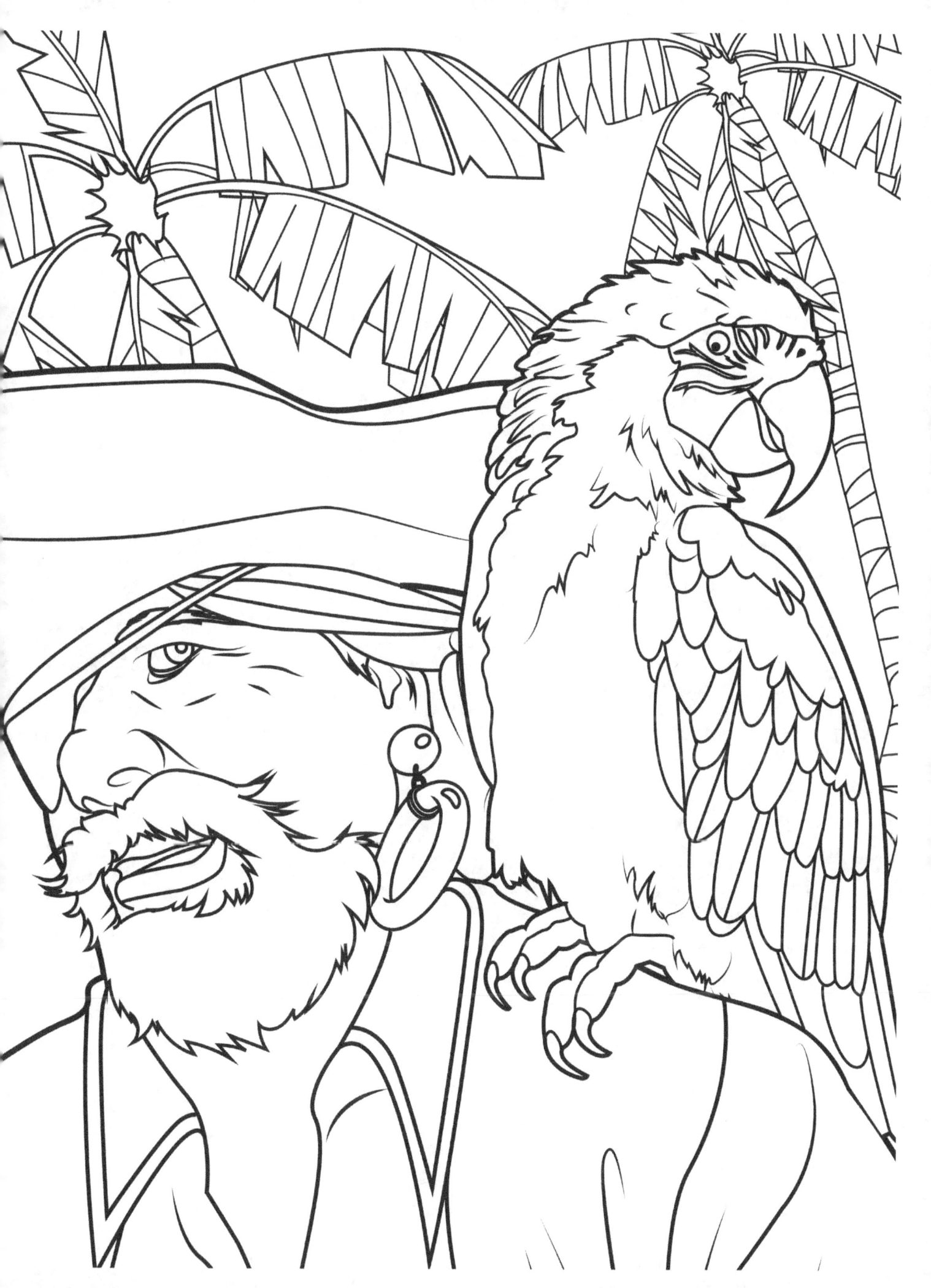

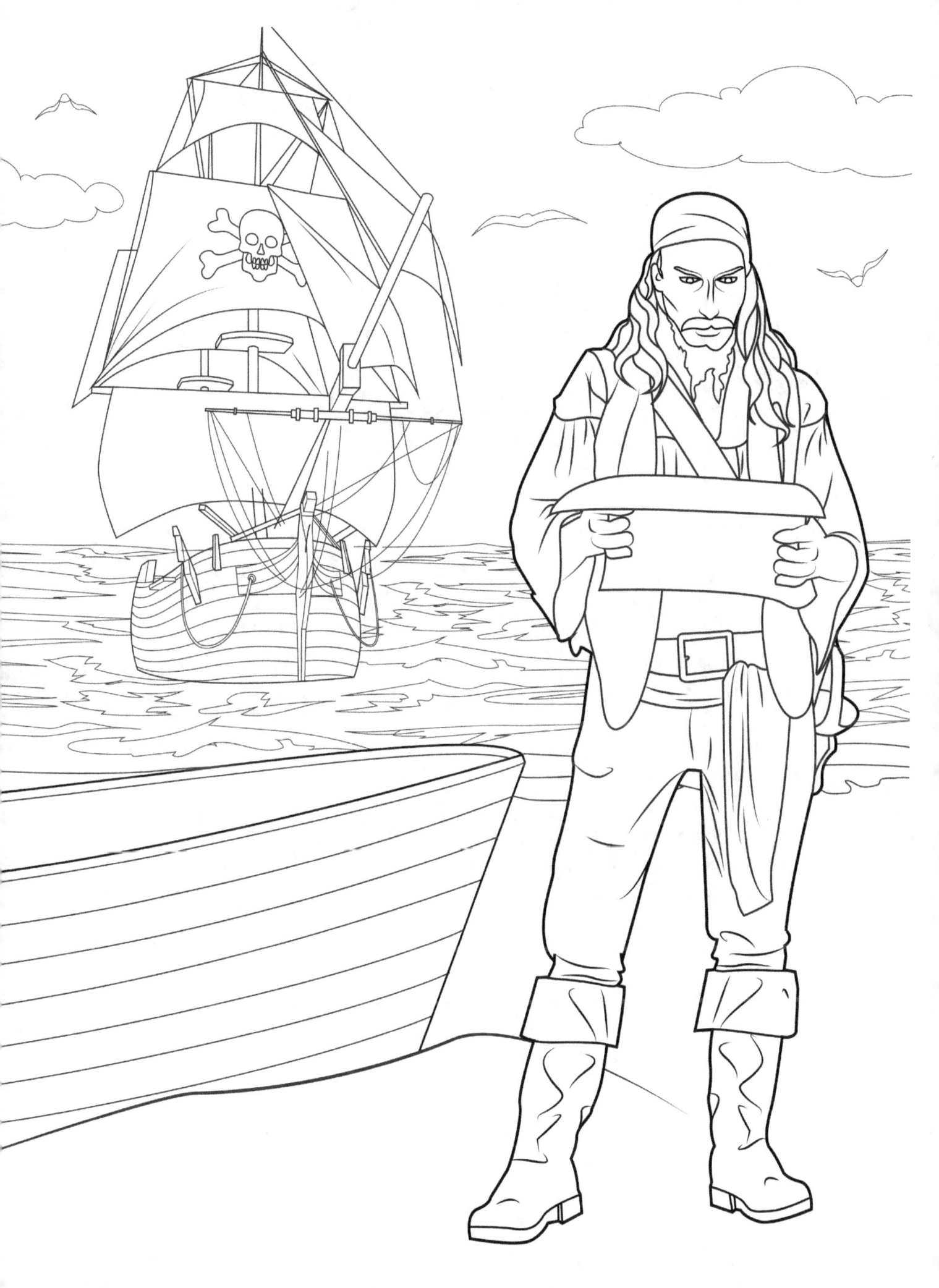

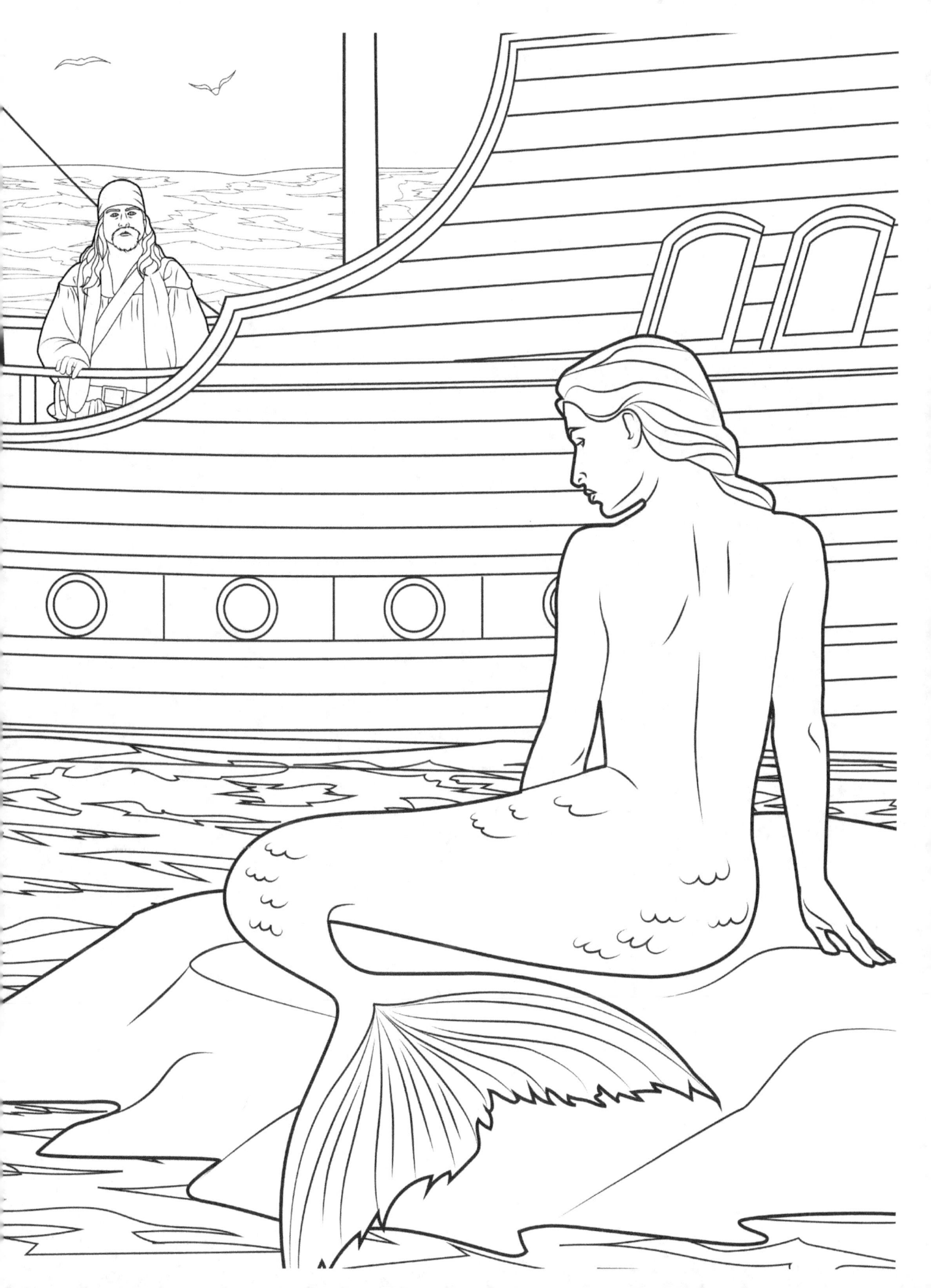

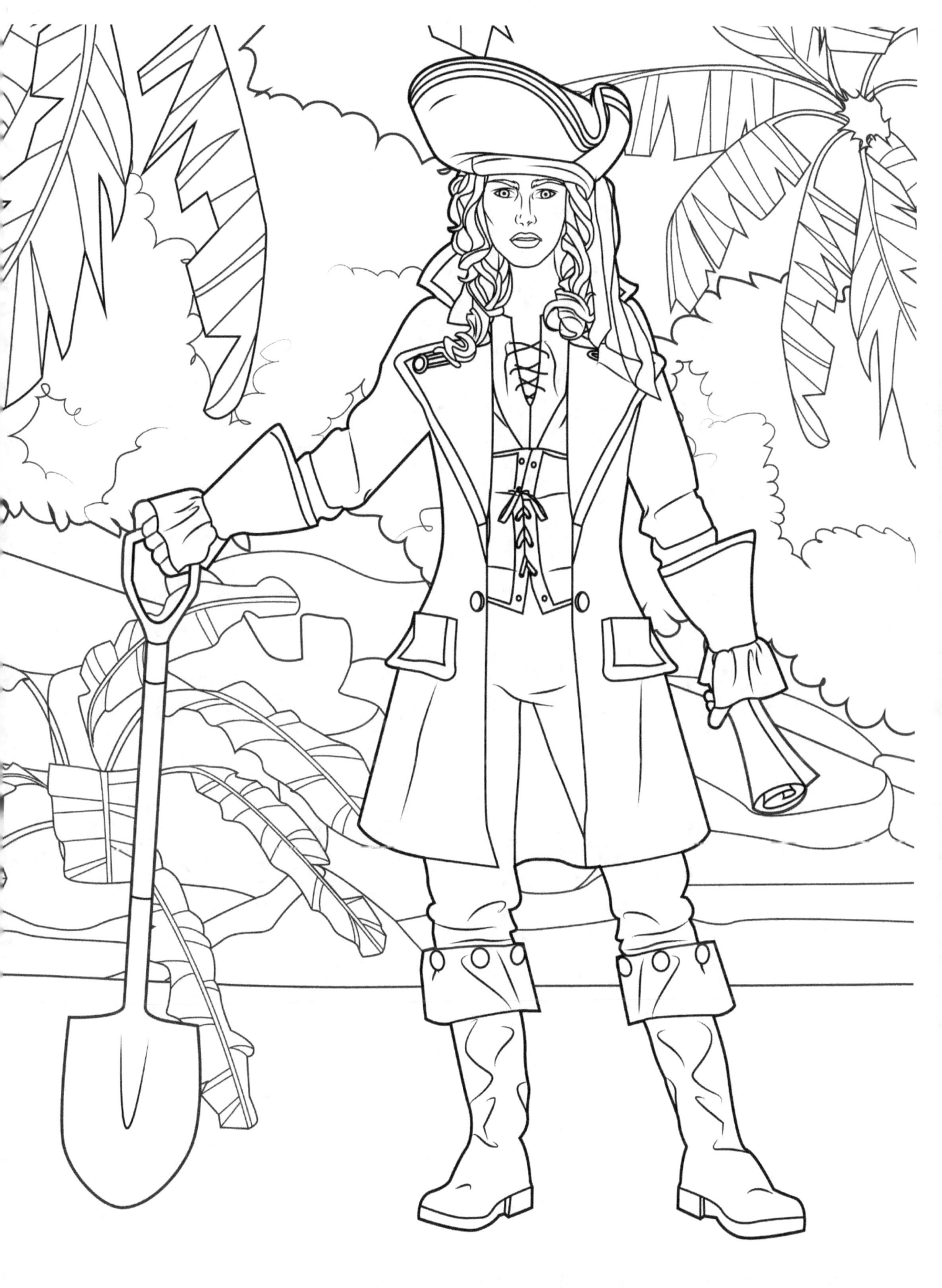

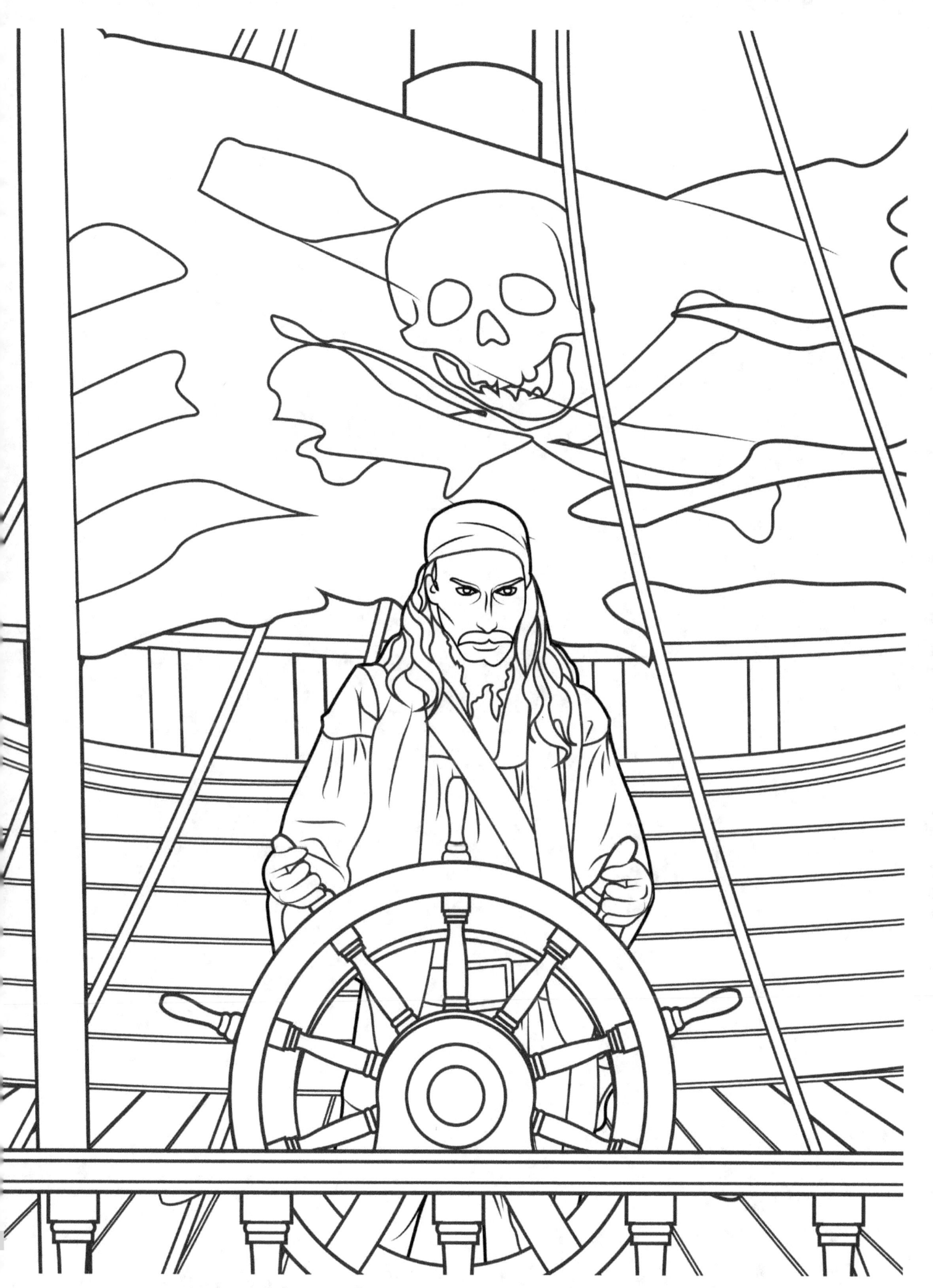

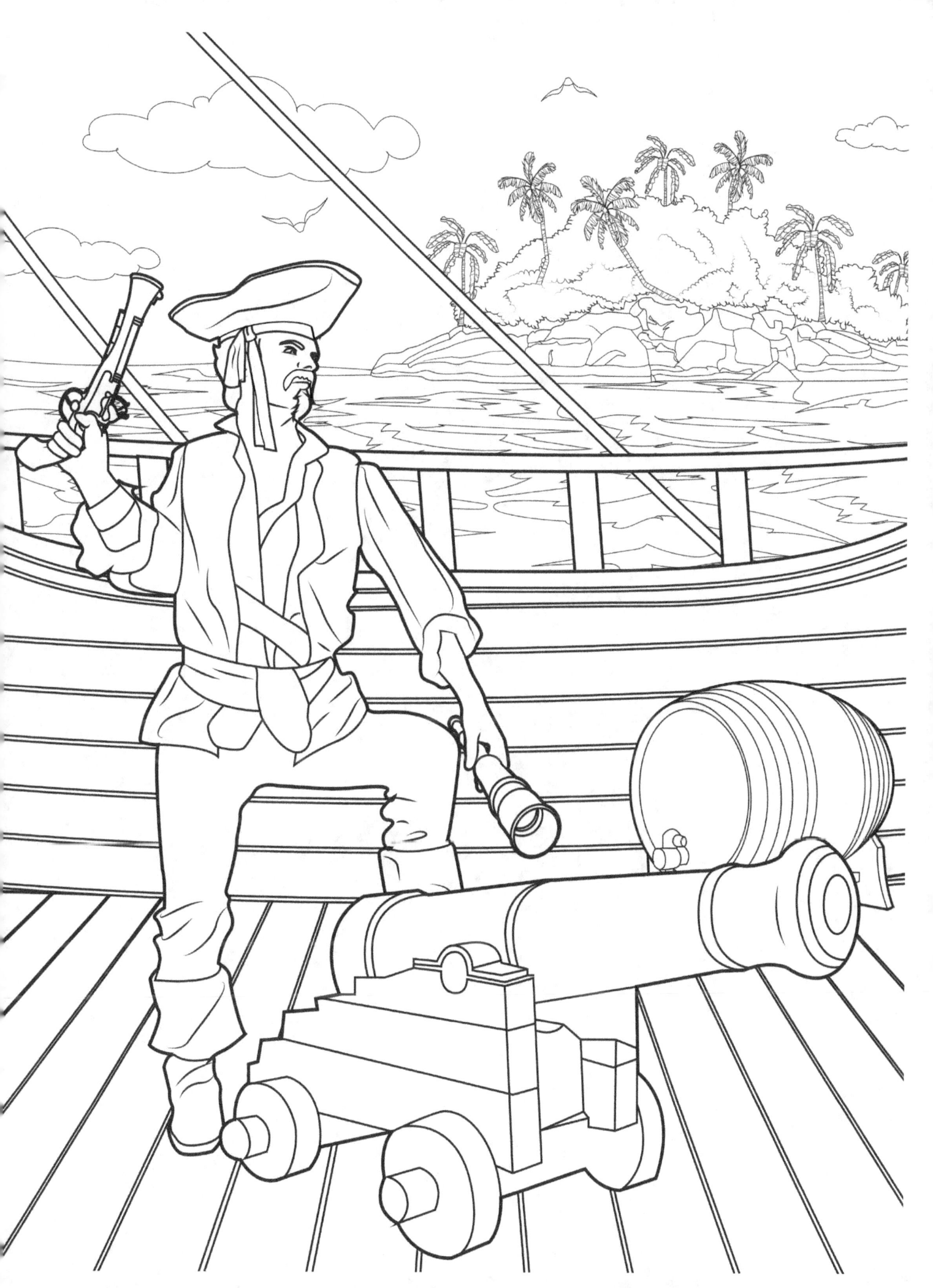

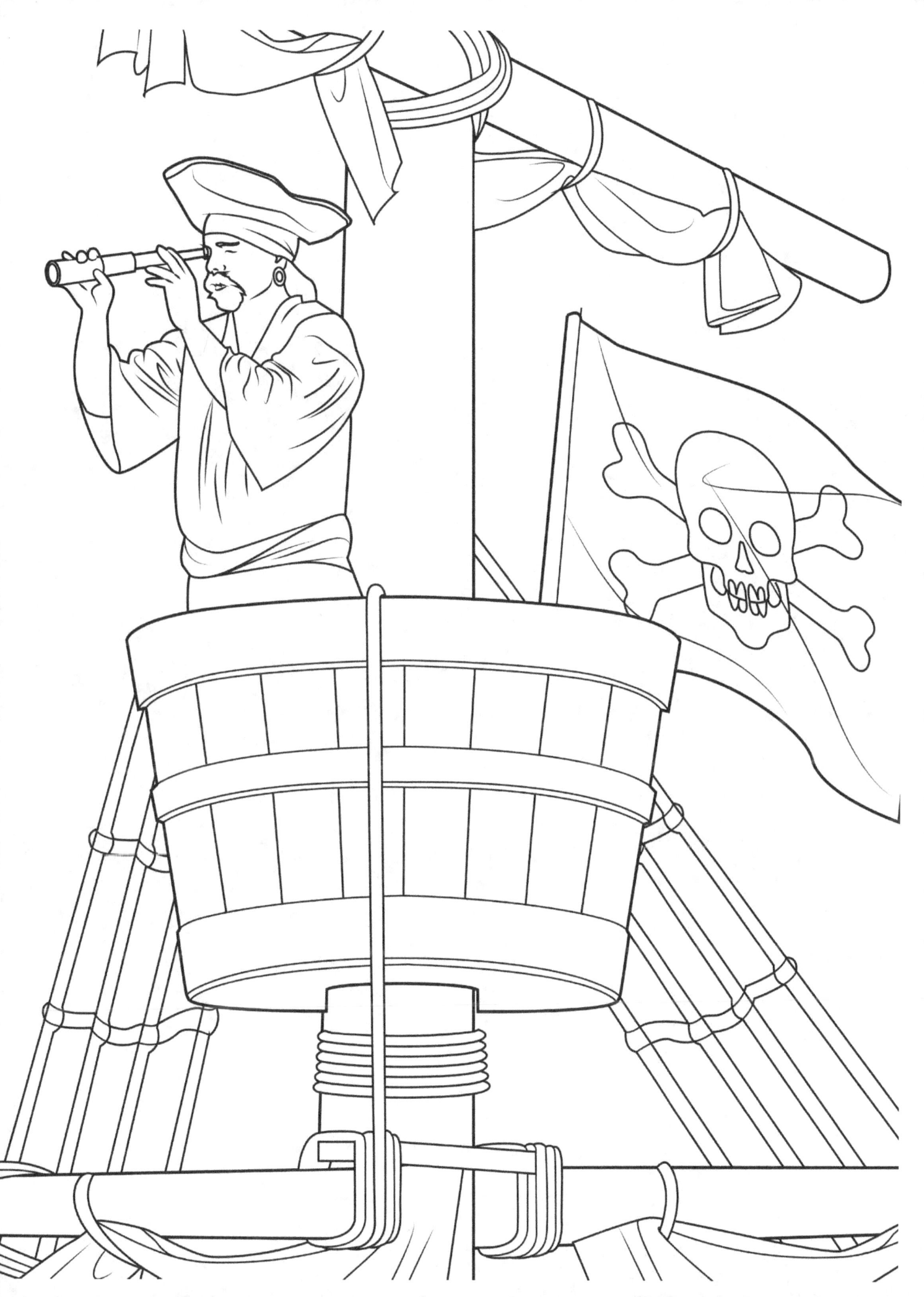

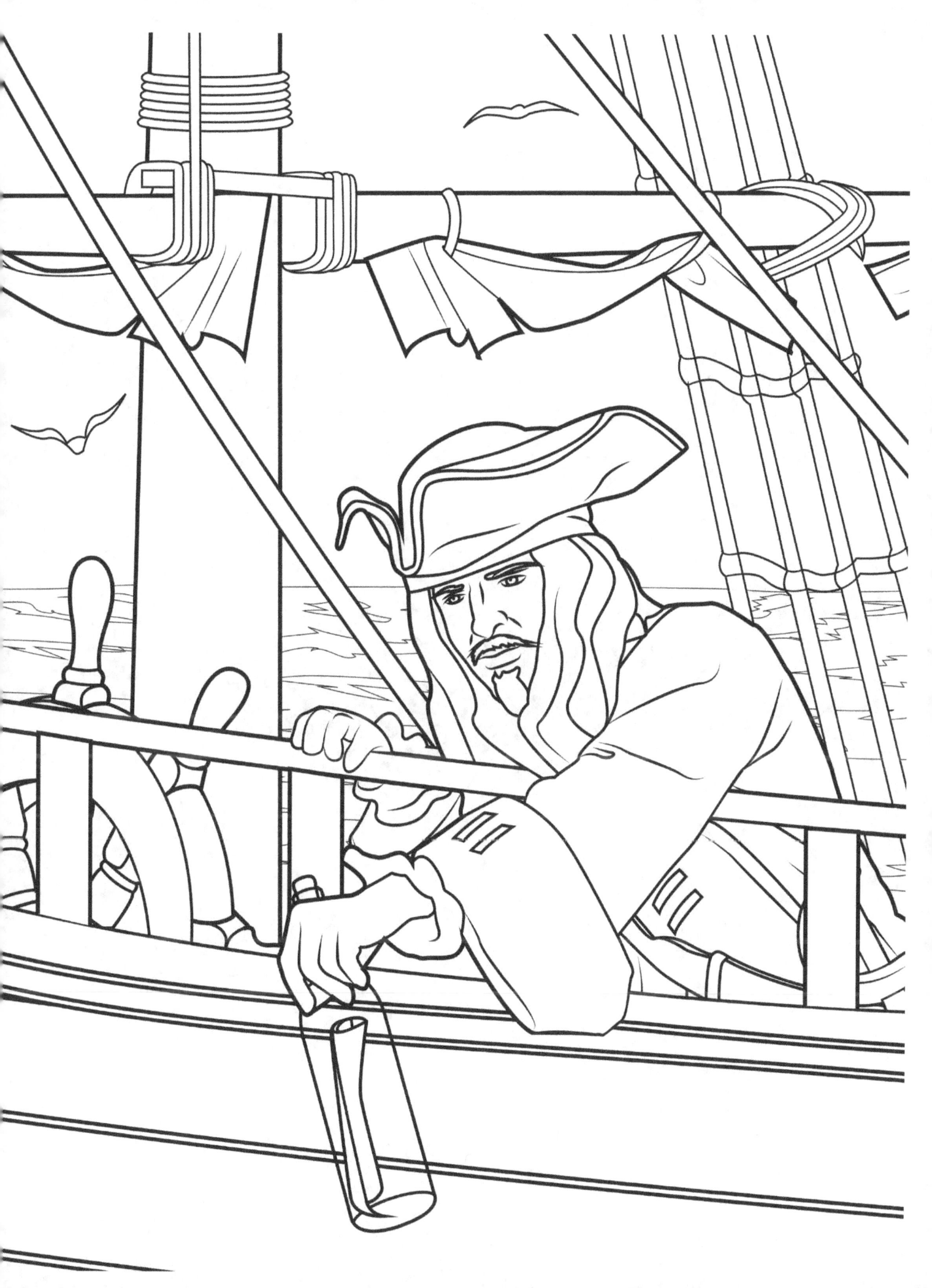

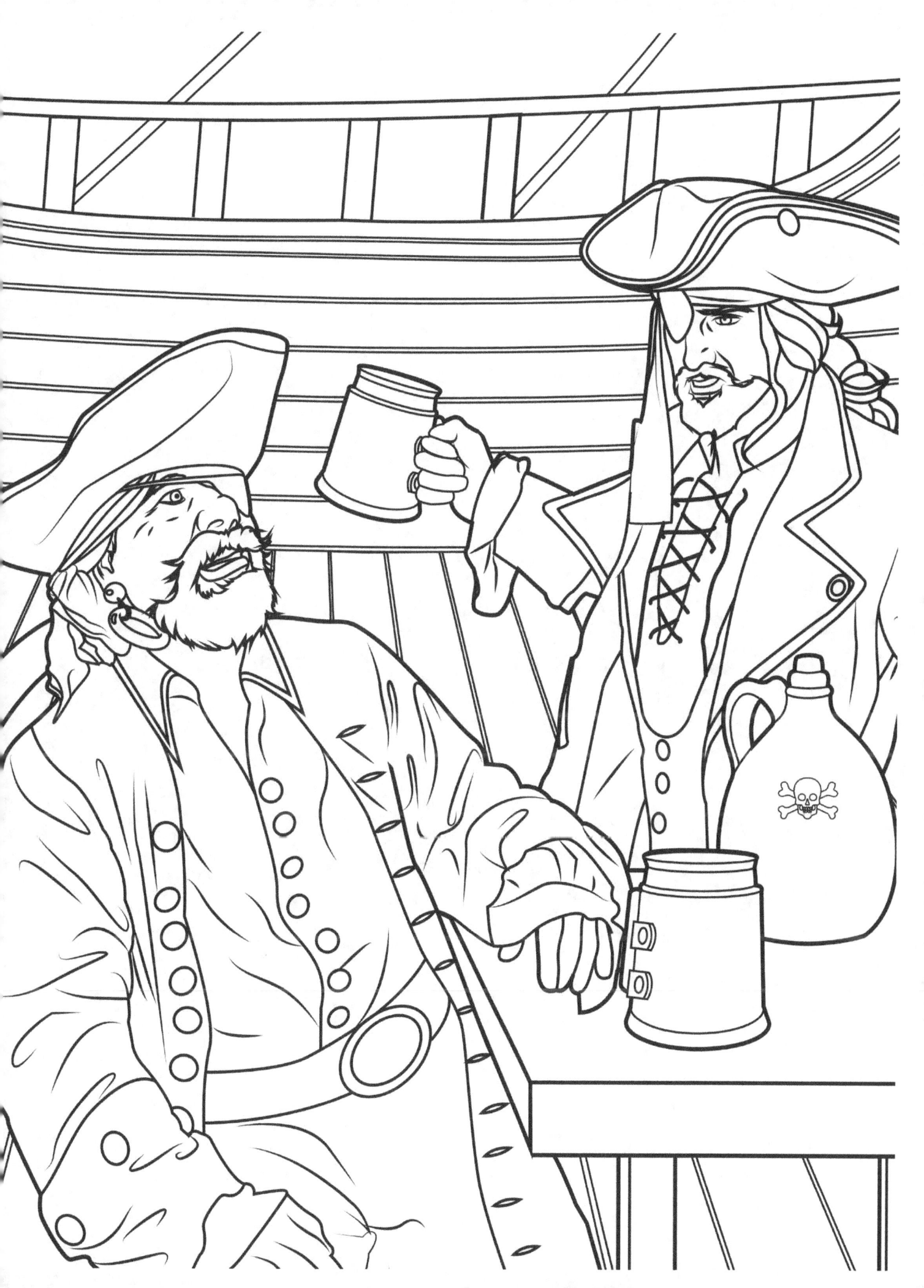

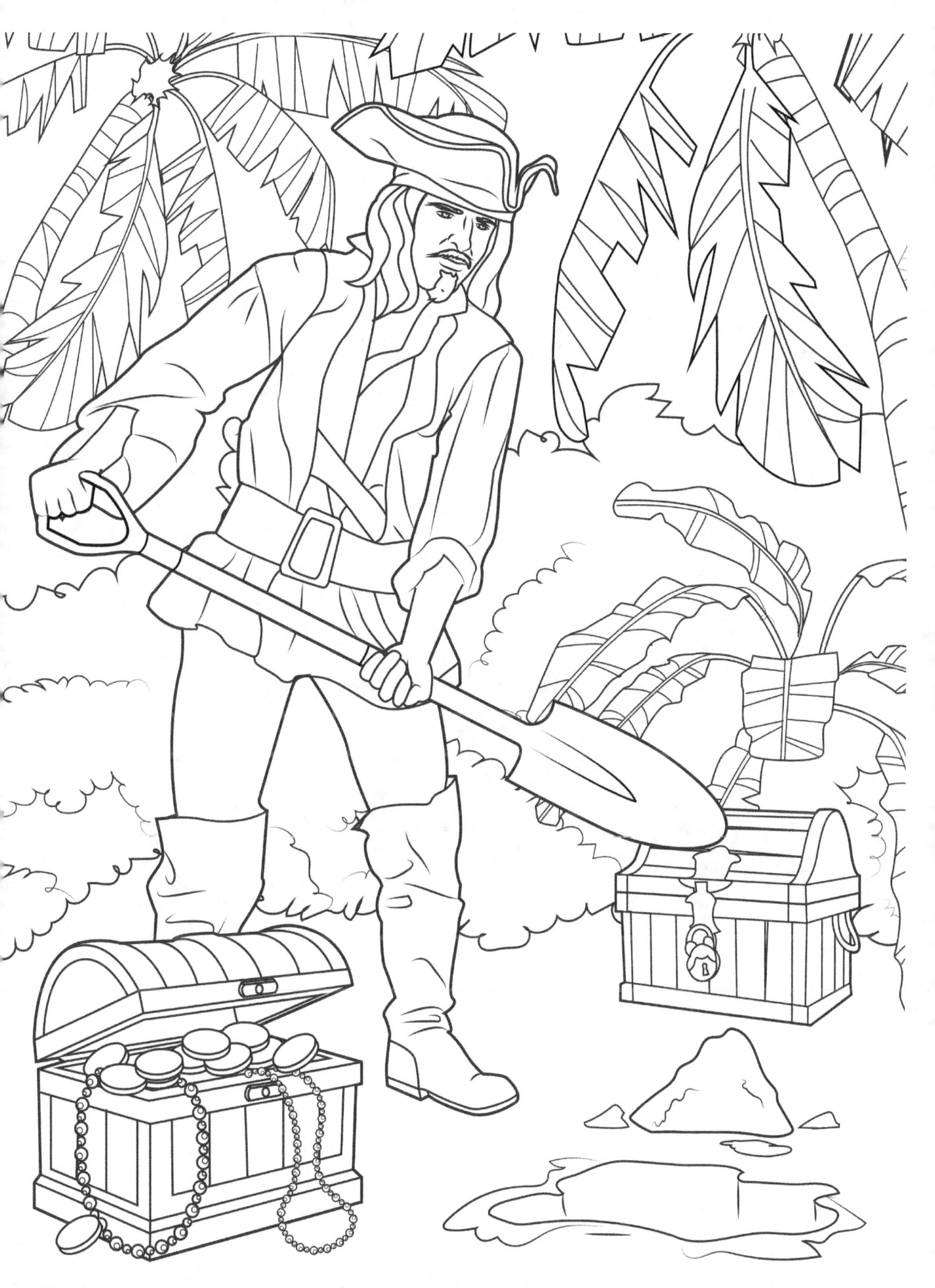

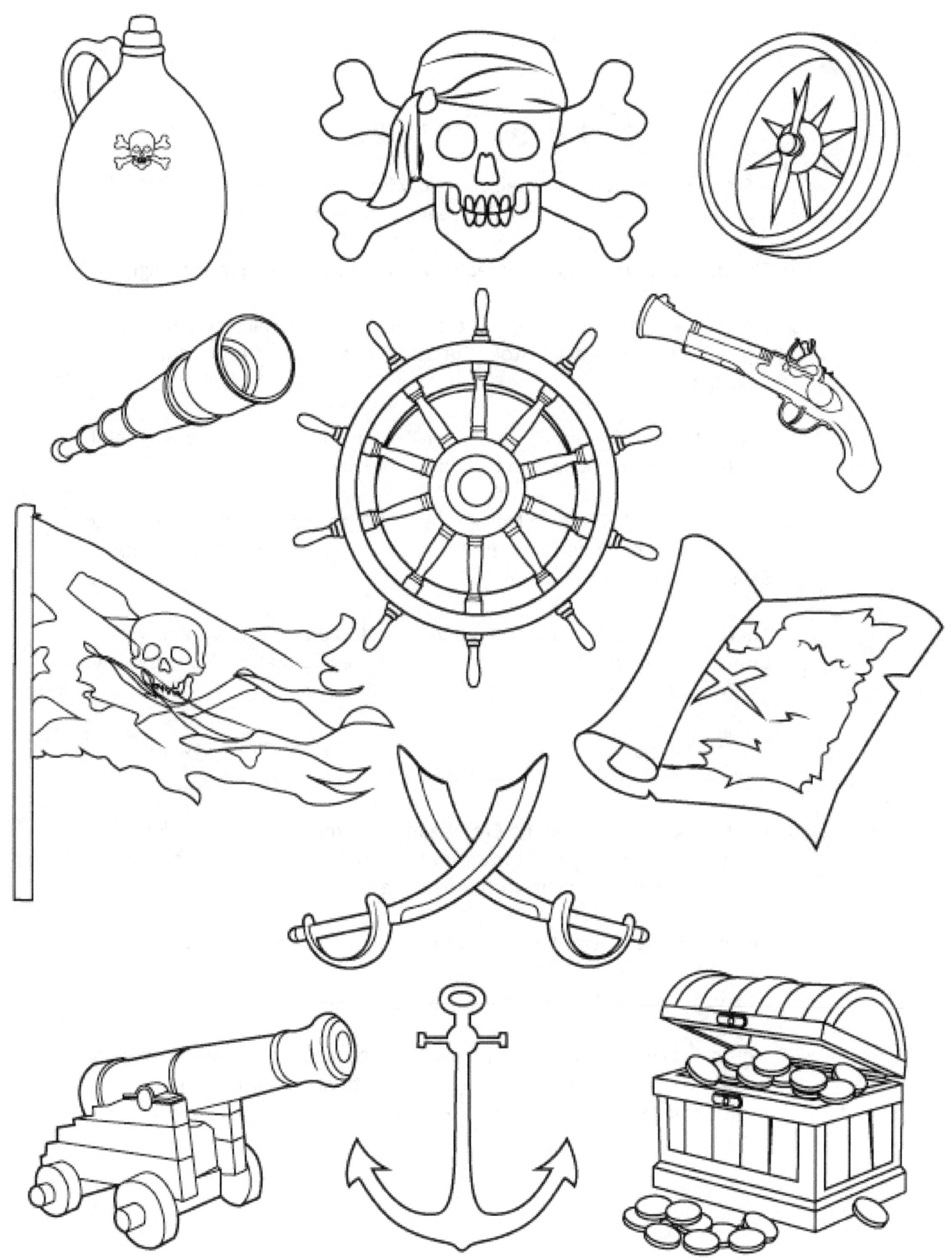

Pirate Facts

1. A Pirate's career didn't usually last very long. In fact, on average, most would only be active for about 2 years, and their average age was 23.

2. The US dollar was originally created at equal value to 1 piece of eight.

3. Pirates used whatever weapons they could lay their hands on, but they typically used Muskets, Pistols, Cutlasses, Grenades, Firepots and Boarding Axes.

4. The first records of piracy come from Ancient Greece, and there are still Pirates active on the seas to this day.

5. One of the worlds leading Universities, MIT, awards certificates in Piracy to students who have completed courses in Archery, Pistol Shooting, Sailing, and Fencing.

6. There is no known record of anyone being forced to walk a plank by a pirate. It's thought that the myth became prevalent after being featured in "Treasure Island".

7. The Golden Age of Piracy, when there was the most pirate activity around the world, was between 1690 and 1730.

8. Pirates who operated in the Caribbean were known as Buccaneers, those who sailed in the Mediterranean were known as Corsairs, and those who were based in North Africa were known as Barbary Pirates.

9. Queen Elizabeth I was known to authorise pirates to fight on England's behalf against enemies. Known as Privateers, they included Sir Francis Drake, Sir George Clifford, and Sir Henry Morgan.

10. No-one has ever found a real pirate treasure map, or at least no-one has admitted to it. Pirates would usually spend their haul quickly and couldn't be certain they'd have the chance to return to where they had left it.

11. Pirate ships operated under a strict code that prevented crew members from fighting with each other, drinking too much rum, or stealing from each other.

12. Anne Bonny was the most famous female pirate. She sailed with Captain Jack Rackham, and became friends with another successful female pirate called Mary Read.

13. Pirates would wear eye patches to help their eyes adjust to light differences. When they went into the cabin from the deck, they would switch the eye that the patch was worn over.

14. Ear Piercings were not worn as a fashion statement. Pirates actually though that they would help to improve their eyesight.

15. It was very unusual for pirates to steal gold, silver, or jewels. The goods that were commonly stolen included tobacco, cotton, wood, sugar, spices, and cocoa.

16. A powerful pirate captain, Benjamin Hornigold, once led his crew into battle to steal hats for themselves. They had thrown their own overboard after a night of drinking rum.

17. The biggest single pirate raid in history took place in 1695. Henry Avery captured an Indian treasure ship called "Ganj-i-sawai" and took jewels and precious metals that would be worth £52 million today.

18. Pirates would often take over towns to make them safe havens for those who broke the law. The most famous of these was Port Royal in Jamaica and the entire island of Tortuga.

19. A pirate ship would have up to 80 crew members, whereas most English ships would only have 30 men on board.

20. Pirate captains were only in charge of the ship and crew during battles. At other times, the crew answered to the ships Pilot who would receive the same share of the bounty as the captain.

Pirate Word Search

Ooh Arr, can you find all of the hidden words?

```
A X S D P F H R Z P Z I O U Q
L N Y T Q X I E O P N P J V L
V P S N R N S E W S M K X B P
Y Q Q G C A P T A I N K I D D
G K X U Z E A A L X O N Q A W
E H T J T B N V K Q N E E V N
T Y D O K B I I T Q N P W Y Q
R M O J R I O R H C A V E J S
P U O O T R L P E D C R G O P
H N A B F A A E P R U M H N T
Z G Y L Y C N P L S I O E E W
D Q A A I R S S A L G Y P S W
H C T A P E Y E N W G P Z O G
H E G I J M R R K E N X C A W
S I M W G T P O H R W Y N S G
```

Cannon   Eye Patch   Rum
Captain Kidd   Hispaniola   Spyglass
Caribbean   Parrot   Treasure
Davy Jones   Privateer   Walk The Plank

Pirate Quiz

1. Who was Jim Hawkins' parrot named after in Treasure Island?
2. What is Davy Jones' Locker?
3. Where would Pirates find creatures called 'Weevils'?
4. Which member of a Pirate crew had the authority to veto the Captain's orders?
5. A Piece of Eight was a Spanish coin forged from which metal?
6. Calico Jack Rackham is credited with designing which pirate flag?
7. In the Pirates of the Caribbean movies, what did Jack Sparrow use to point him in the direction of the thing he wanted most in the world?
8. What is the name of the comic opera by Gilbert and Sullivan that featured pirates?
9. In the famous song, how many men are "on the dead man's chest"?
10. What was the name of Captain Pugwash's ship?
11. A lack of which Vitamin will cause scurvy?
12. What did it mean if a ship flew the "Yellow Jack" flag?
13. Which Pirate town did an earthquake destroy in June of 1692?
14. What was the name of the Pirates who were authorised by countries to raid the ships of their enemies?
15. Captain Woodes Rogers drove Pirates off which Caribbean island?
16. What is celebrated every year on the 19th of September?
17. If you were known as a "Jonah", what would you be thought to bring to the ship?
18. What was the average length (in feet) of the cannon used on Pirate ships?
19. What was the most popular name for a Pirate ship?
20. Which Pirate earned the most money in his lifetime?

Pirate Crossword

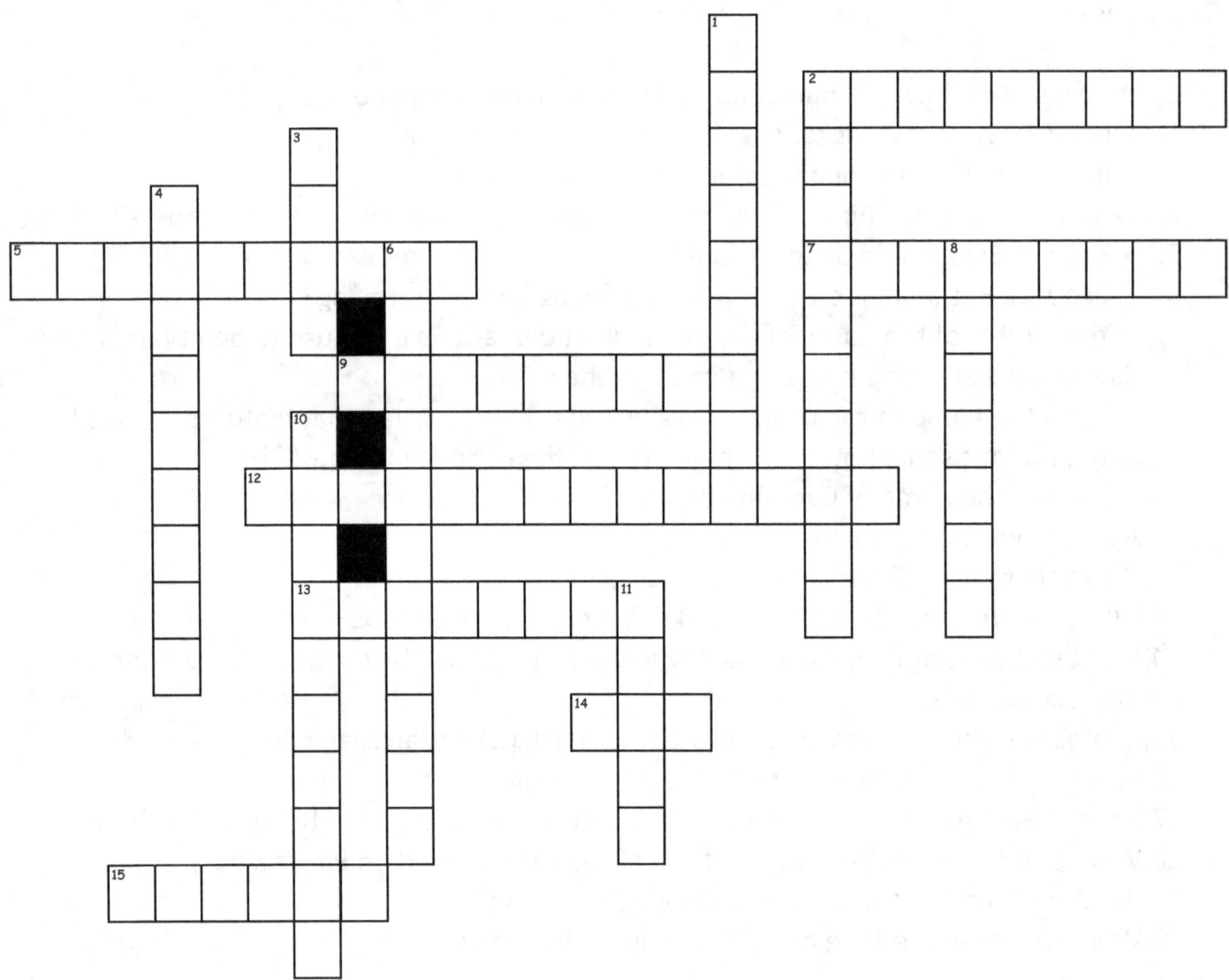

Across

2. Another word that meant Pirate in the West Indies (9)

5. The name of the famous Pirate flag (5,5)

7. Where the Lookout of the ship stands (5,4)

9. Captain Hook was petrified of this animal (9)

12. The name of the legendary Ghost Ship (6,8)

13. The name given to Pirates of the Mediterranean (8)

14. How Pirates remember where they buried their treasure (3)

15. Shiver me _____ (7)

Down

1. First name of the English monarch who encouraged Pirates to attack her enemies (9)

2. The name of Jack Sparrow's ship in Pirates of the Caribbean (5,5)

3. A Pirate's favourite drink made from Rum, Water, Lemon Juice and Sugar (4)

4. The Pirate who is thought to have captured more than 400 ships in 4 years (5,4)

6. What did Pirates wear because they thought it would improve their eyesight? (3,8)

8. What were you not allowed to do on a Pirate ship for fear of turning the weather stormy? (7)

10. The nickname of the notorious Pirate Edward Teach (10)

11. The country whose treasure ships were often plundered by Pirates in the Caribbean (5)

Spot The Difference

6 Differences to Spot. Can You Spot Them All?

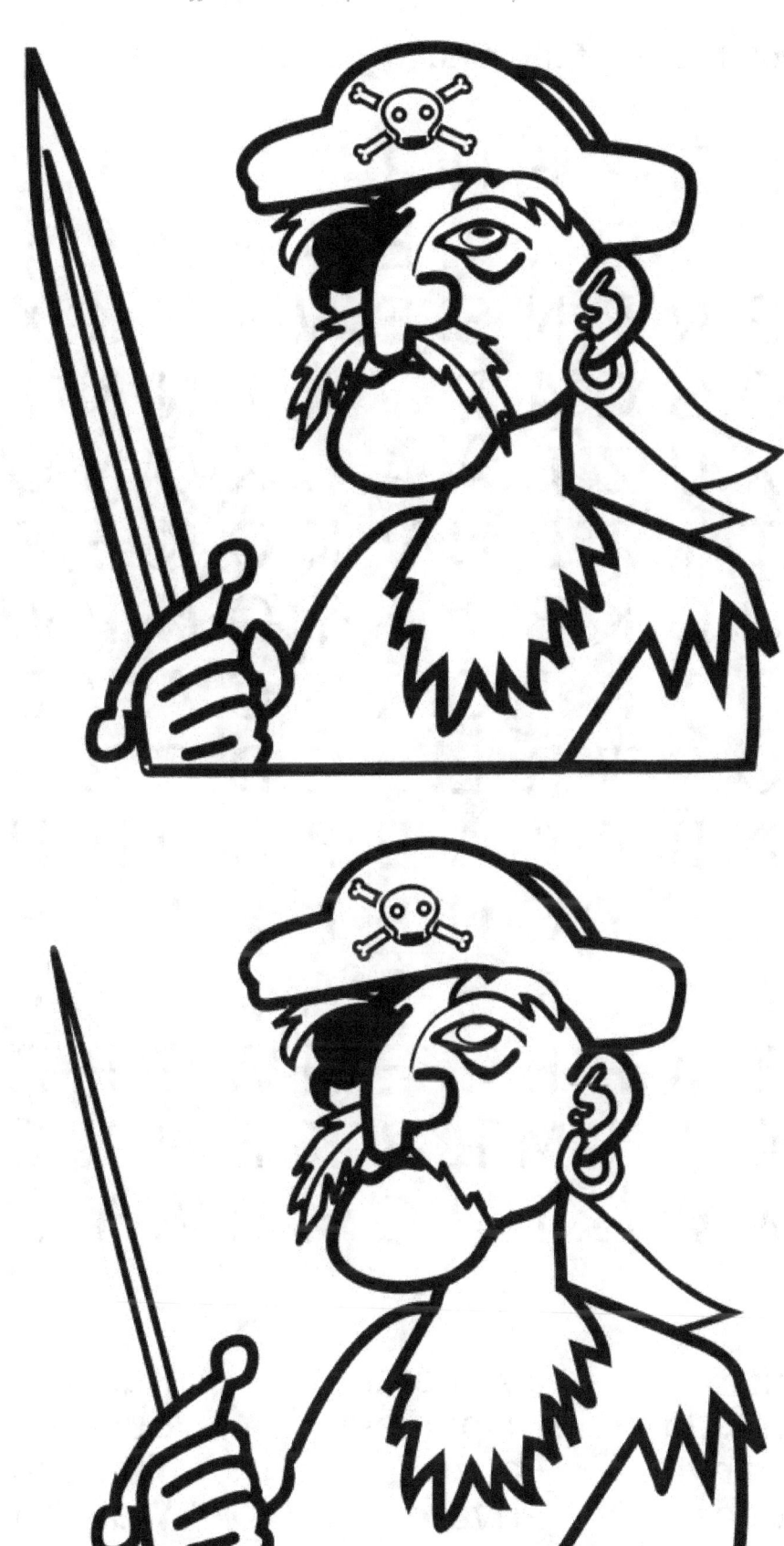

Pirate Word Search

Ooh Arr, can you find all of the hidden words?

```
A X S D P F H R Z P Z I O U Q
L N Y T Q X I E O P N P J V L
V P S N R N S E W S M K X B P
Y Q Q G C A P T A I N K I D D
G K X U Z E A A L X O N Q A W
E H T J T B N V K Q N E E V N
T Y D O K B I I T Q N P W Y Q
R M O J R I O R H C A V E J S
P U O O T R L P E D C R G O P
H N A B F A A E P R U M H N T
Z G Y L Y C N P L S I O E E W
D Q A A I R S S A L G Y P S W
H C T A P E Y E N W G P Z O G
H E G I J M R R K E N X C A W
S I M W G T P O H R W Y N S G
```

Cannon	Eye Patch	Rum
Captain Kidd	Hispaniola	Spyglass
Caribbean	Parrot	Treasure
Davy Jones	Privateer	Walk The Plank

Answers

1. Captain Flint
2. The bottom of the sea
3. In their food stores
4. The Quartermaster
5. Silver
6. The Jolly Roger
7. A supernatural compass
8. The Pirates of Penzance
9. Fifteen
10. The Black Pig
11. Vitamin C
12. There was an illness aboard the ship
13. Port Royal in Jamaica
14. Privateer
15. The Bahamas
16. International Talk Like a Pirate Day
17. Bad Luck
18. 7 Feet
19. Revenge
20. Samuel "Black Sam" Bellamy (Who earned the equivalent of $130 million in todays money)

Spot The Difference

1. Bone from the Skull and Crossbones
2. Top Piece of Bandana
3. Left Moustache
4. Pupil
5. Thumb
6. Sword

Other Coloring Books from Aryla Publishing

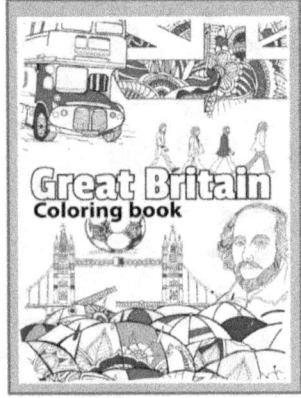
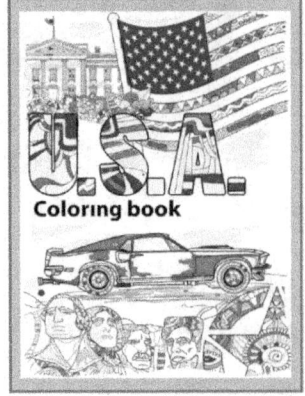
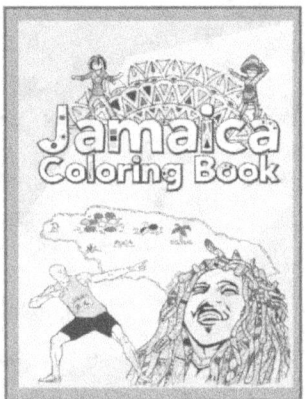
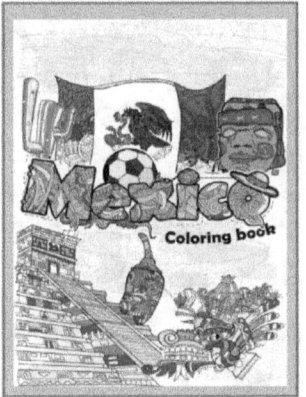

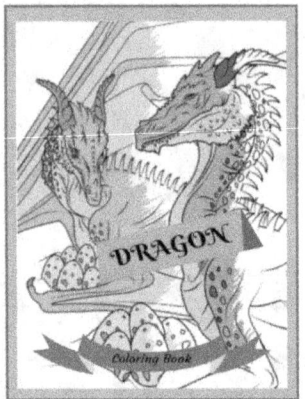
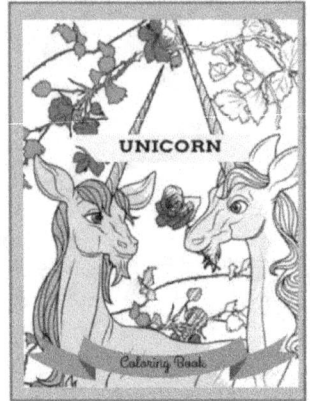
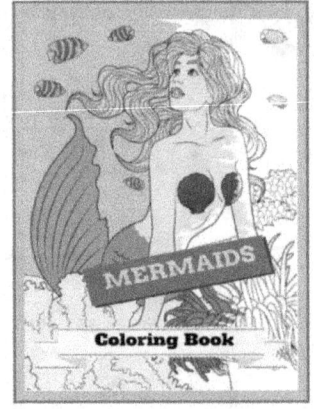
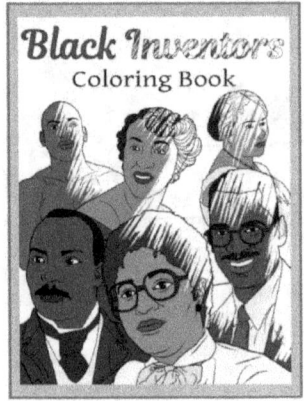
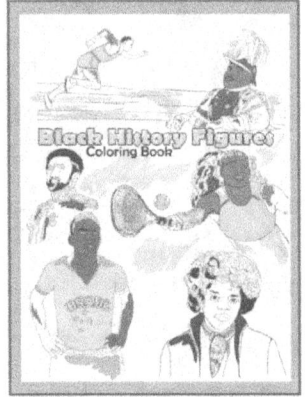
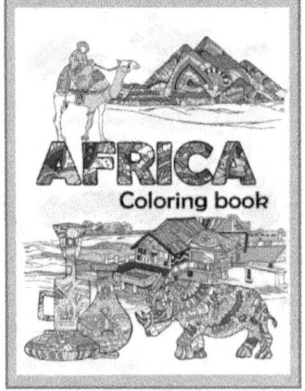
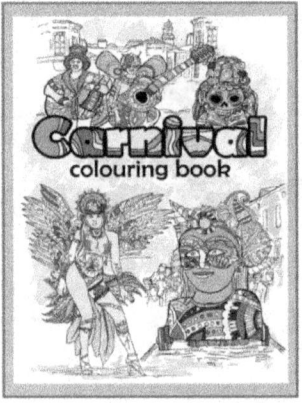
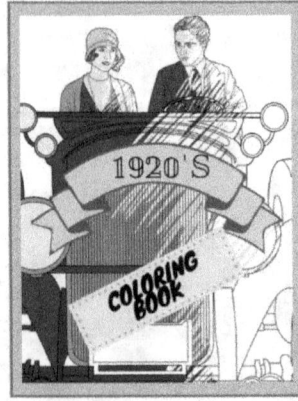
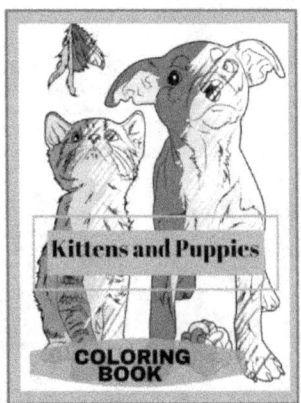
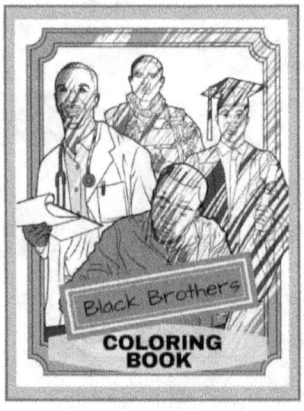
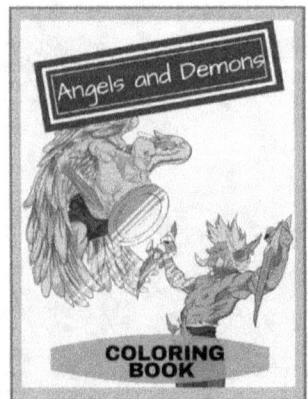

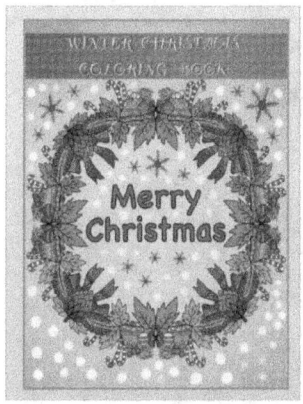
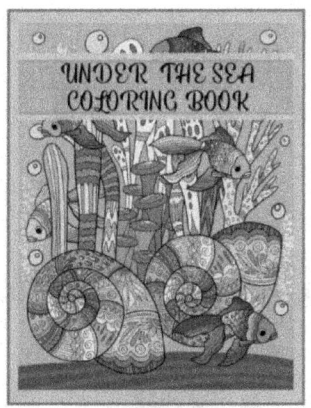
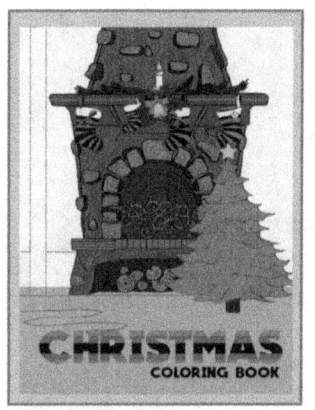
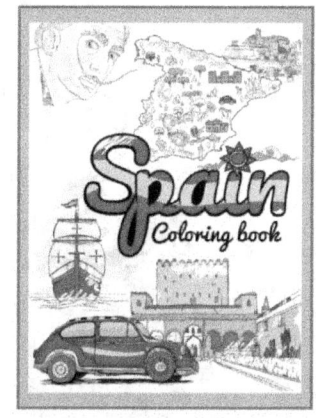
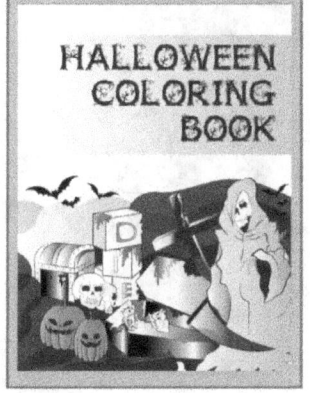
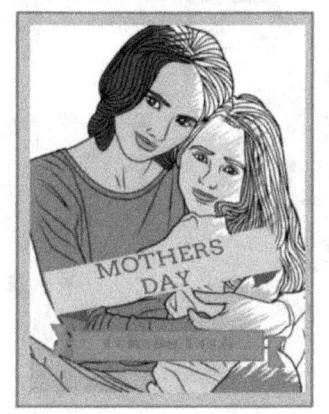
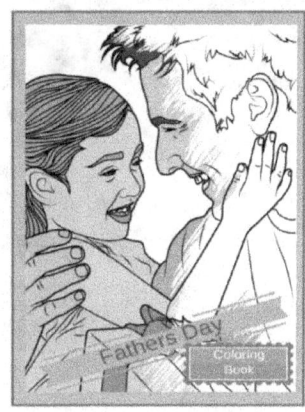
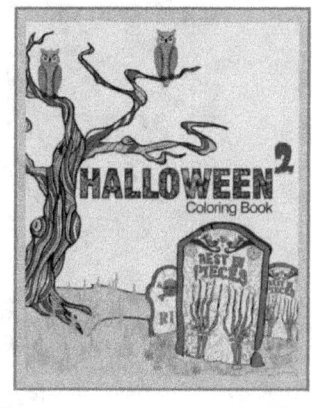
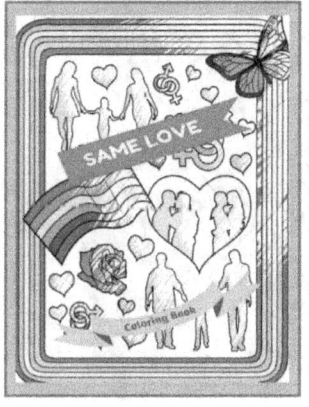
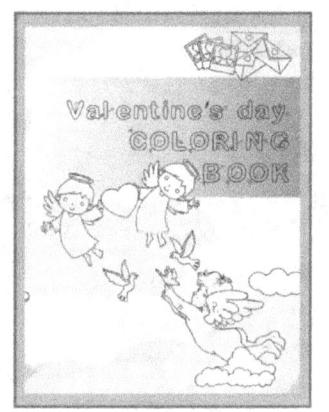
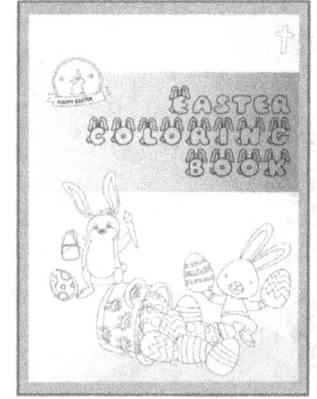
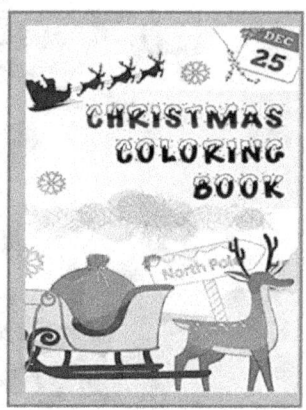
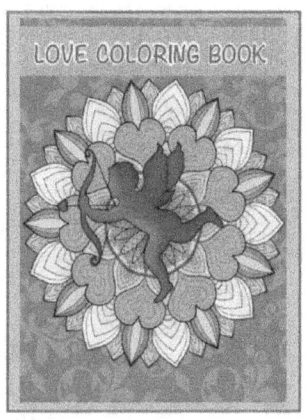
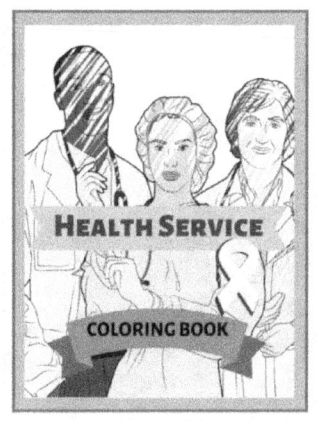
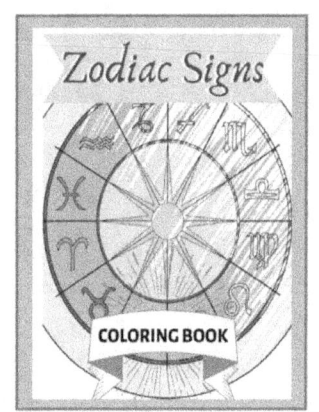
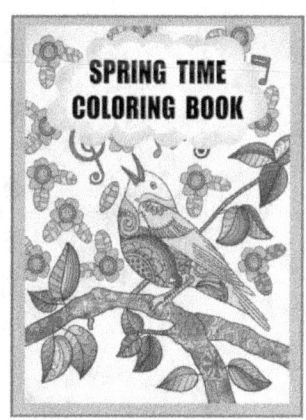

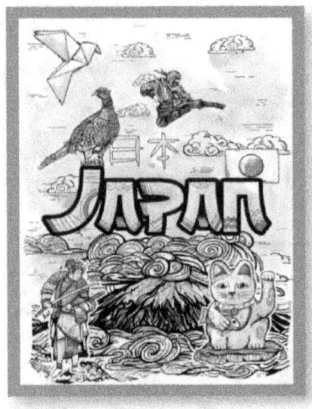

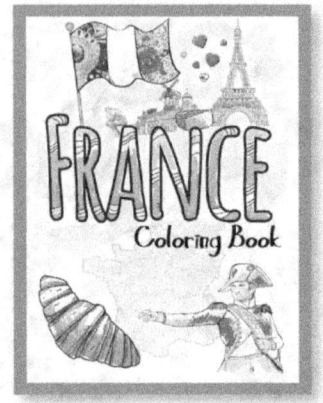

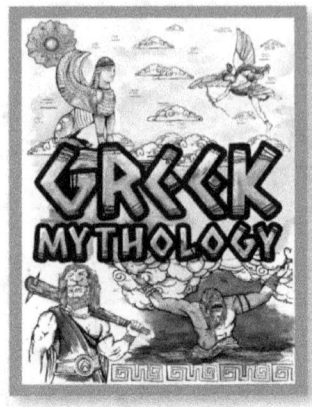

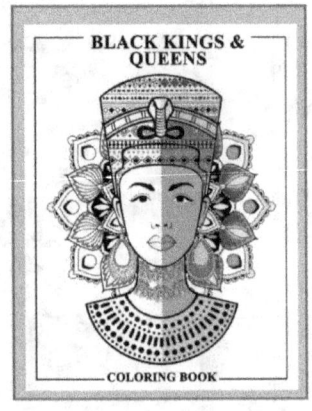

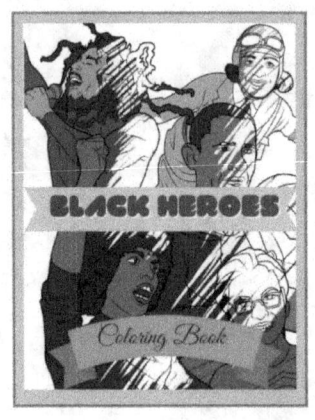

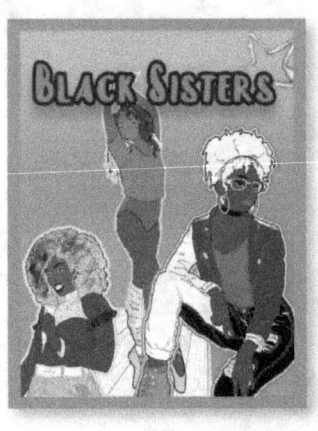

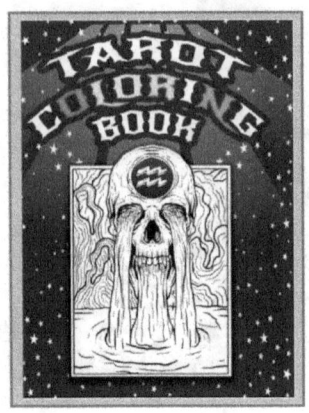

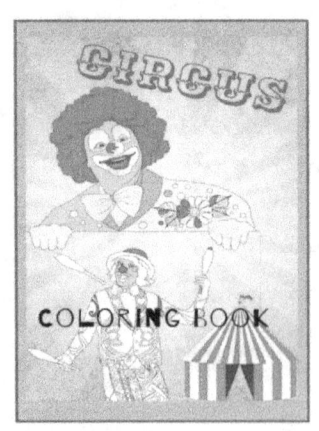

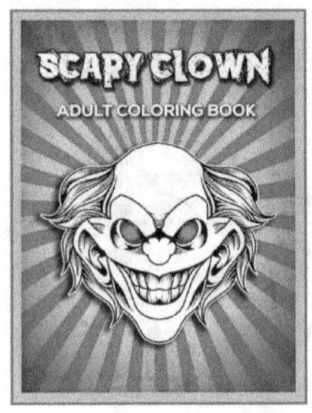

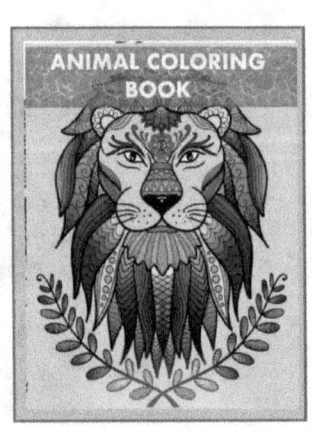

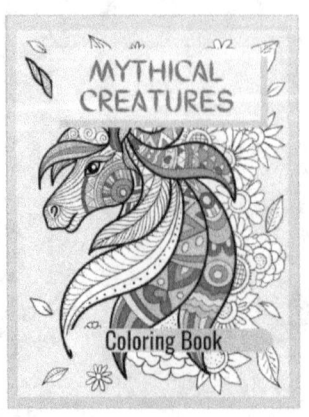

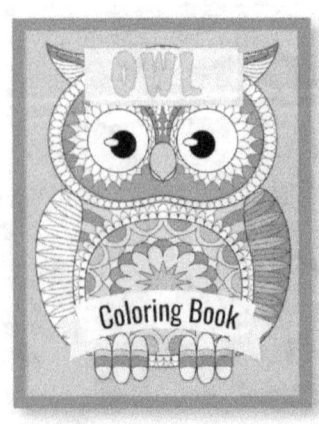

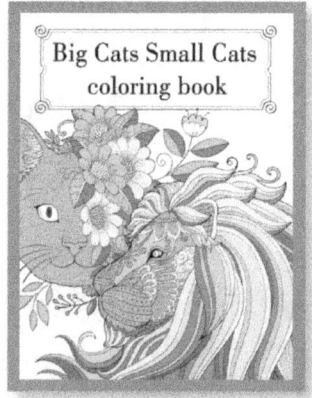

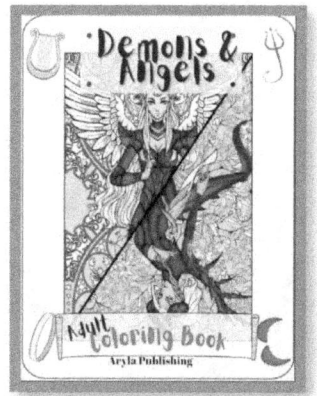

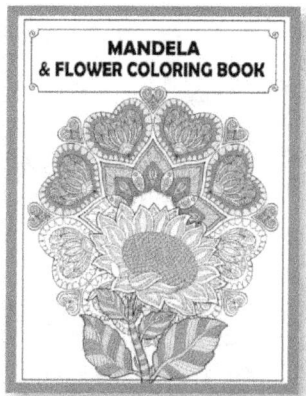

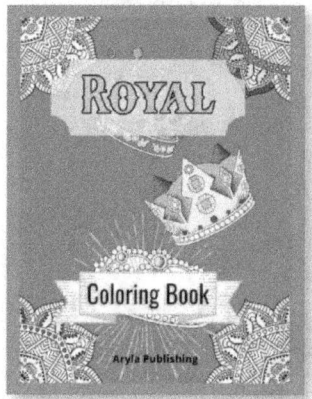

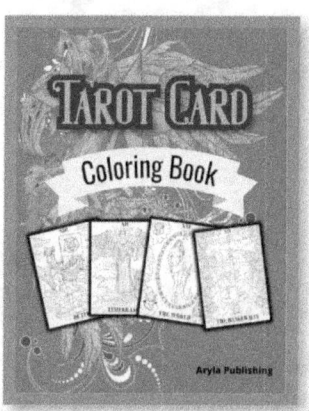

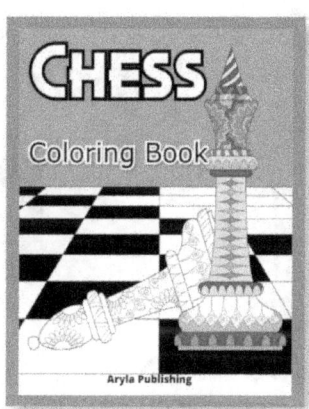

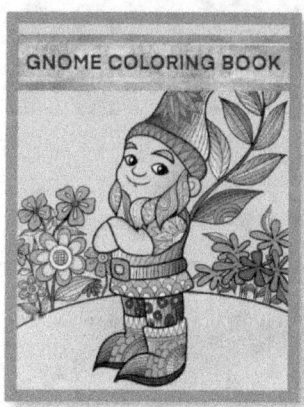

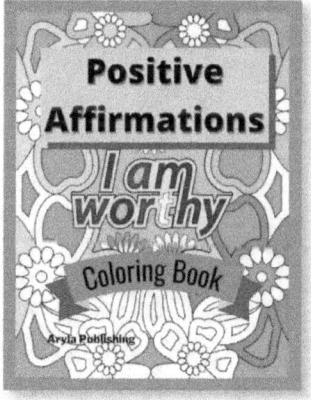

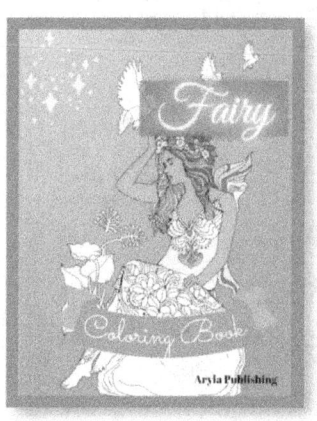

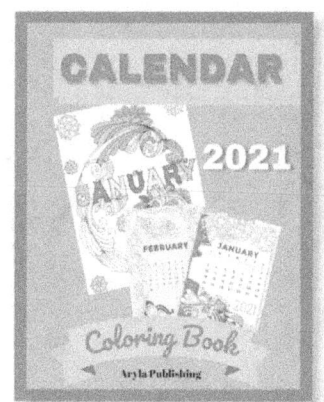

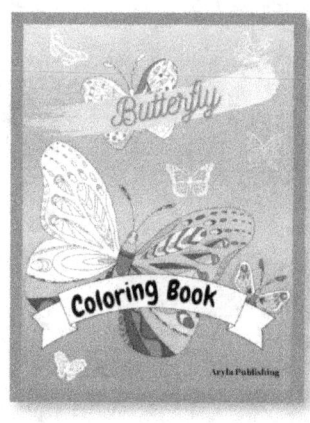

Color In Fun
Kids Books

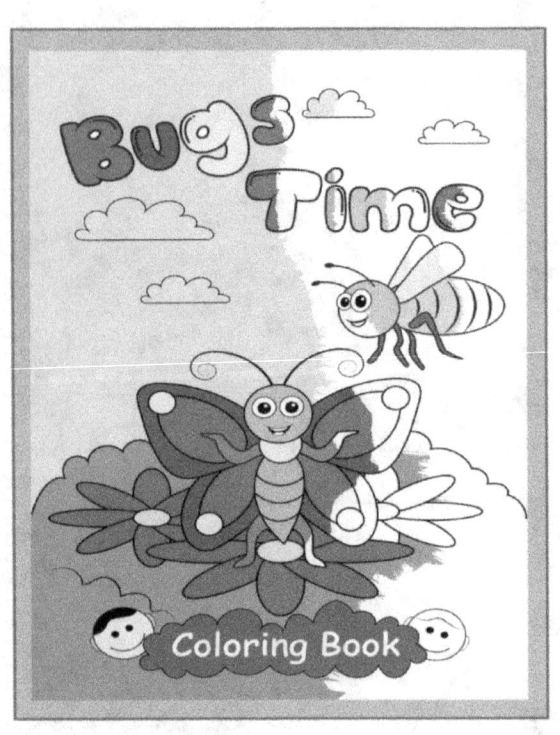

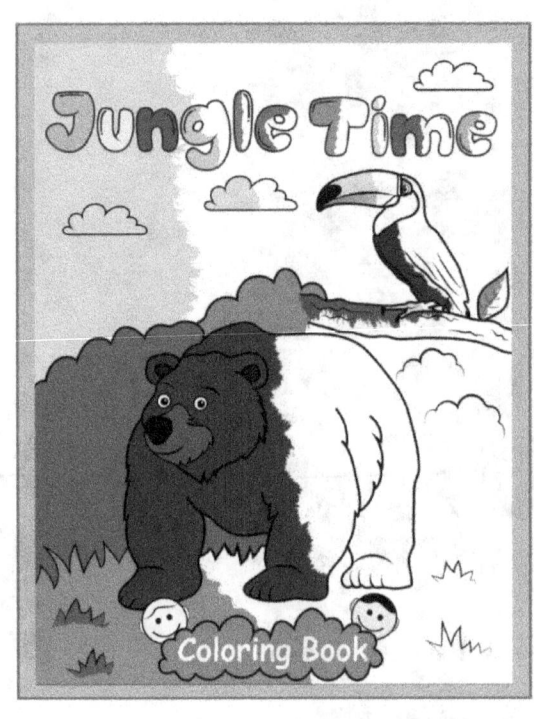

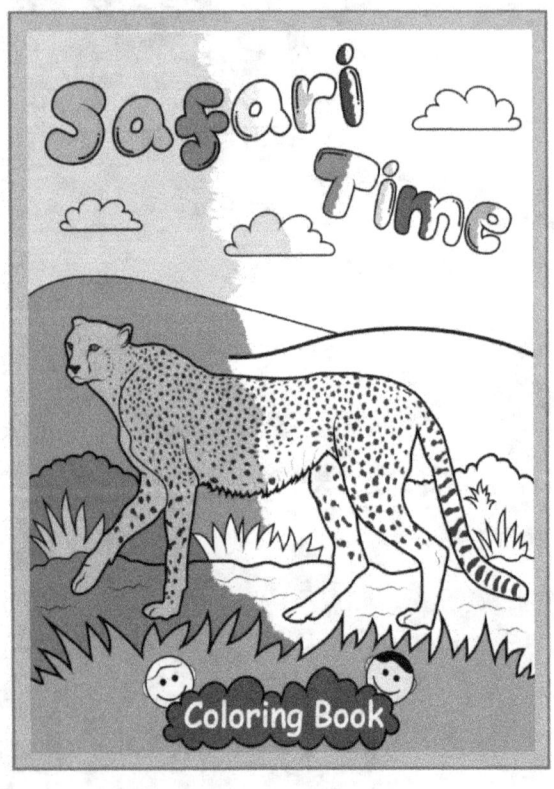

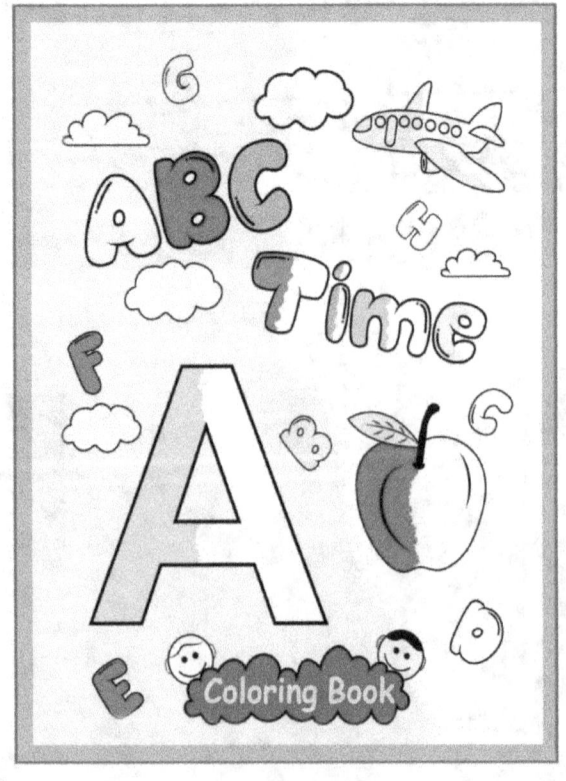

Thank you for purchasing this book.

If you would like to know more about Aryla Publishing Books please visit:-

www.ArylaPublishing.com

Or follow us on
Facebook
Twitter
Instagram
for *free promotions*

@arylapublishing

We would love to know what you think of this book so please leave us a review.

Have a wonderful day ☺

Visit **www.ArylaPublishing.com**

to find out about all new releases.

Follow us @arylapublishing on Twitter Instagram & Facebook

  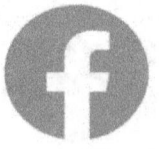

Search for Aryla Publishing on

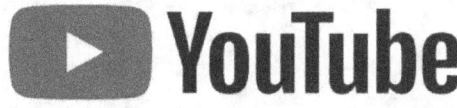 **YouTube**

Check out our Book Trailers

Subscribe to keep up to date with new releases!

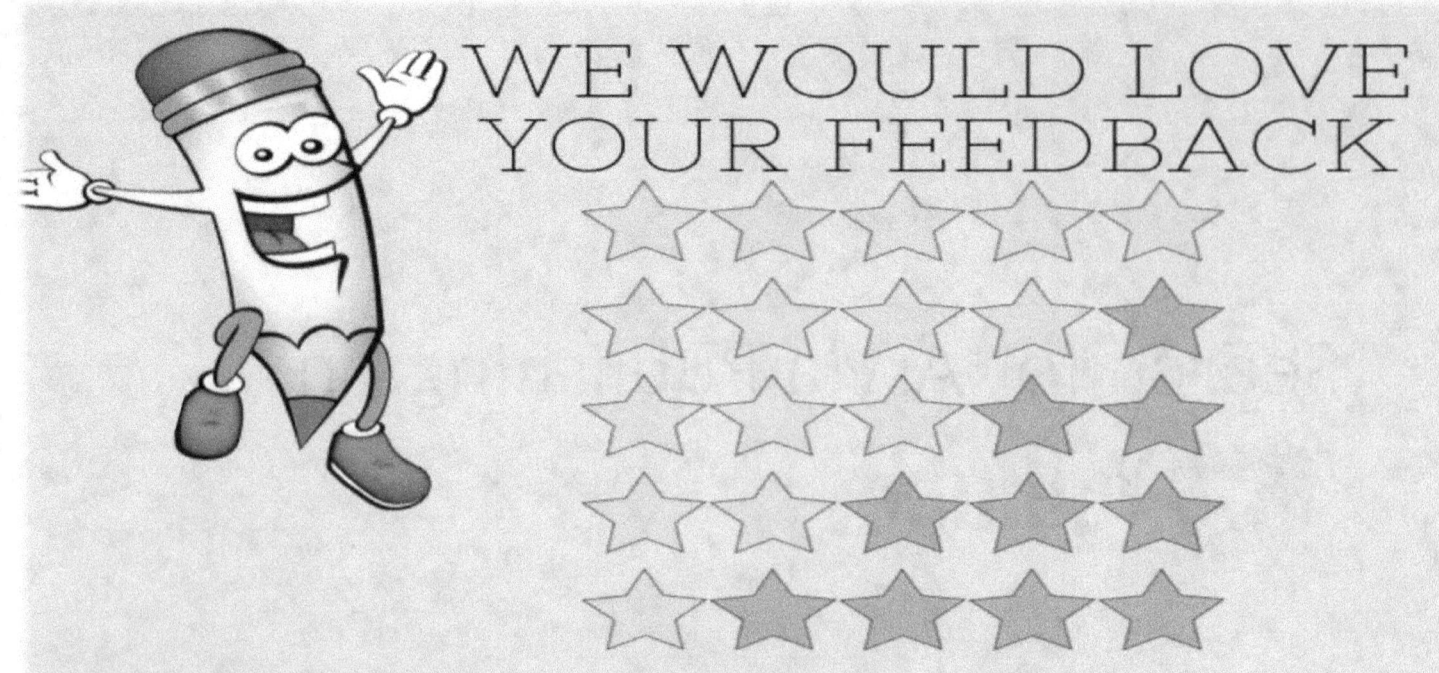

WE WOULD LOVE YOUR FEEDBACK

PLEASE LEAVE REVIEW AT:-

https://review.arylapublishing.com/pirate

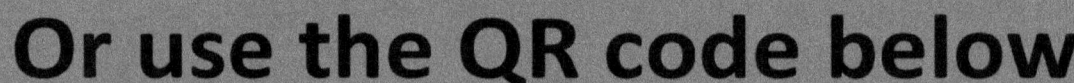

Or use the QR code below

www.ingramcontent.com/pod-product-compliance
Lightning Source LLC
Chambersburg PA
CBHW081749220526
45468CB00008B/2298